Confessions of an Adulterous Christian Woman

Lies that got me there
Truths that brought me back

• Lyndell Hetrick Holtz •

BEACON HILL PRESS
OF KANSAS CITY

Copyright 2007
By Lyndell Hetrick Holtz

ISBN-13: 978-0-8341-2328-1
ISBN-10: 0-8341-2328-2

Printed in the United States of America

Cover Design: Lindsey Rohner
Interior Design: Sharon Page

Library of Congress Cataloging-in-Publication Data

Holtz, Lyndell Hetrick, 1954-
   Confessions of an adulterous Christian woman : lies that got me there, truths that brought me back / Lyndell Hetrick Holtz.
      p. cm.
   Includes bibliographical references.
   ISBN-13: 978-0-8341-2328-1 (pbk.)
   ISBN-10: 0-8341-2328-2 (pbk.)
   1. Adultery. 2. Sex—Religious aspects—Christianity. 3. Lust—Religious aspects—Christianity. 4. Marriage—Religious aspects—Christianity. 5. Holtz, Lyndell Hetrick, 1954- I. Title.

   BV4627.A3H65   2007
   241'.66092—dc22

                                        2007024368

10   9   8   7   6   5   4   3   2   1

Contents

Foreword   5

Introduction   7

1. The Road to Ruin   11

2. Proceed with Caution   19

3. Sharp Curves Ahead   27

4. The Road of Turmoil and Confusion   35

5. The Detour to Rebellion   45

6. No Turnaround Back to Eden   55

7. Accident Ahead   63

8. Only One Way Back Home   71

9. Who Is Carrying the Mountain?   81

10. The False God Eros   93

11. The Tragedy of What Might Have Been   119

12. Restoring the Vision of God's Glory   143

13. Now or Never: Promised Land or Wilderness?   167

Special Prayers   189

Notes   191

For my husband, David,
whose love and forgiveness
perfectly mirrors our God of second chances.

Foreword

Writing openly about our failures is difficult to do. But Lyndell Holtz is willing to open the window on her experiences with a transparency that will lead to transformation.

As she shares each step on her path to moral failure, we are alerted to constantly be on guard against setting foot on a slippery slope that ends in tragedy for us and the ones we hold dear.

But God is in the business of redemption, and it is His joy to do awesome things in our lives. From the abyss of adultery to the blinding light of His love and faithfulness, Lyndell's openness reminds us of our Father's grace and mercy.

Lyndell's journey allows you to glimpse the Light that seeks you regardless of your circumstances. A Light that will penetrate your heart, revealing its darkest corners and saturating you with redemptive truth.

Thank you, Lord, for your mercies that are new every morning.

Joyce Williams

Introduction

In May of 2004 I stood at the edge of the Grand Canyon for the very first time. As the setting sun wrapped me in a golden glow, a soft breeze floated up from the canyon's depths and caressed my face. It was an unforgettable moment of pure beauty. Tears rolled down my face, not only because of the grand miracle of nature that stretched before me, but also because it was a miracle that I was even standing there along with my husband and a group from our church on a spiritual/leadership retreat. Gratitude was exploding inside me for what God had done in my life, for the Creator of all things beautiful had allowed beauty to grow once again to replace the emptiness of my own making. Exactly four years earlier, my life had collapsed. I had turned to adultery as an escape from an unhappy life. As a result, the life I had known and all that I held dear had vanished with no hope of recovery.

As I faced the damaging winds of sorrow and loss because of my sin, Satan had a field day. My husband of 25 years, who had pastored for 20 years, divorced me due to my infidelity. I had been a public school teacher, a Sunday School teacher, the mother of four, and the oldest daughter of faithful Christian parents. With grim finality, our marriage ended in anger and bitterness, and my former husband moved to another state.

Mere words cannot convey my sorrow, sense of loss, and my shame. I was alone, stripped of all dignity, with the accuser's voice taunting me: "How could you have done that? You are worthless—God will never forgive you for what you did. Some Christian you turned out to be!" But into this pit of absolute despair and brokenness, God stooped down.

My purpose in telling my story is twofold. First, to serve as a warning. Adultery brings enormous loss and untold pain. Second, I tell my story to hold out hope to you as I lift up the One who is able to redeem, restore, and rebuild broken lives. For the husband who stood beside me at the rim of the Grand Canyon was the man I had betrayed eight years earlier. Nearly three years after our separation and subsequent divorce, God called us back to our marriage. With a dramatic intervention and then slow, steady progress, God rebuilt our relationship. Sin is not an impossible foe for God, and He longs to prove that this is true.

I certainly don't claim to have all the answers. I claim only my many mistakes and God's grace. My desire is that you will apply to your own life the truths God gave in my darkest hour.

The story of my descent is not easy to tell, but I rejoice in telling of His power and redeeming love that transformed a broken and ruined life. In adultery, I found neither the miraculous nor the awesome; rather, the result was failure and abomination before God.

Today I can only marvel at the power that took me from utter despair to the relentless devotion of Jesus Christ. I hope that you will be touched by His power in this story of grace.

But Jesus went to the Mount of Olives. At dawn he appeared again in the temple courts, where all the people gathered around him, and he sat down to teach them. The teachers of the law and the Pharisees brought in a woman caught in adultery. They made her stand before the group and said to Jesus, "Teacher, this woman was caught in the act of adultery. In the Law Moses commanded us to stone such women. Now what do you say?" They were using this question as a trap, in order to have a basis for accusing him.

But Jesus bent down and started to write on the ground with his finger. When they kept on questioning him, he straightened up and said to them, "If any one of you is without sin, let him be the first to throw a stone at her." Again he stooped down and wrote on the ground.

At this, those who heard began to go away one at a time, the older ones first, until only Jesus was left, with the woman still standing there. Jesus straightened up and asked her, "Woman, where are they? Has no one condemned you?"

"No one, sir," she said.

"Then neither do I condemn you," Jesus declared. "Go now and leave your life of sin."

—John 8:1-11

1

The Road to Ruin

I took a road once that had posted at its beginning: Dead End. I took the road because it didn't *look* like a dead-end road. Silly, I know. I rationalized that pranksters had placed the sign there. I had driven south on a long, country road and now I wanted to go back north without traveling the same road. This road went north, so I took it. I cruised down this scenic country road, confident that I was right and the sign was wrong.

Many miles later, the road came to a dead-end, proving me dead wrong. "You've got to be joking," I said to the cows munching grass where the rest of the road should have been.

When you and I take a wrong road in life, it's really quite like this experience. There are signs at the beginning, but we ignore them because we think we know best. Once we get on the wrong road, we just cruise along, throwing caution to the wind. We litter the road with the feelings of the people we love, our morals, our faith, our values. We toss them right out the window. All we care about is the road and where we believe it is taking us. How dismayed we are when we come to the end and realize the road has betrayed us. It has led us far away from all that was dear and familiar. And we realize that we are not only at the end of the road but also hopelessly lost.

❊ ❊ ❊

This is a good analogy for my life. Two years earlier, during a very difficult time in my life, an innocent friendship slowly and insidiously became an affair. The intense emotions of the affair drove me wildly and blindly down a road I once believed I was incapable of traveling. For a year and a half I struggled to end the relationship, breaking it off only to resume it several weeks later. It was an addiction I seemed to be incapable of breaking. But in May of 2000, it came to an end when my husband discovered my affair, and it was dragged out in the open for all to see. Five months later, my husband divorced me and moved to another state.

The road I was on dead-ended abruptly with divorce. I had ignored God's every warning that adultery was a dead-end road; I had crossed every moral boundary. I screeched to a halt at the edge of a wilderness I had not anticipated. I was consumed with loss and pain and shame.

> Can a man scoop fire into his lap without his clothes being burned? Can a man walk on hot coals without his feet being scorched? *(Prov. 6:27-28)*.

The answer is no. Adultery, like nothing else, consumes your inner and outer life and leaves you standing scarred in its ashes.

I had littered the road to adultery with my beautiful home, traditions I cherished, my 25-year marriage, my Christian witness, precious friendships, my *walk* before my children. Ruin was all around me.

Who was this woman who had traveled to this place, who had taken the road that led her to ruin when all the while she knew better?

> Wisdom calls aloud in the street, she raises her voice in the public squares; at the head of the noisy streets she cries out, in the gateways of the city she makes her speech: "How long will you

simple ones love your simple ways? How long will mockers delight in mockery and fools hate knowledge? If you had responded to my rebuke, I would have poured out my heart to you and made my thoughts known to you. But since you rejected me when I called and no one gave heed when I stretched out my hand, since you ignored all my advice and would not accept my rebuke, I in turn will laugh at your disaster; I will mock when calamity overtakes you—when calamity overtakes you like a storm, when disaster sweeps over you like a whirlwind, when distress and trouble overwhelm you" *(1:20-27)*.

Only when I faced calamity did I carefully scrutinize the signs I had ignored. Only then did I heed the words that would take me home again.

As God and I traveled back over the road that led to adultery and the ruin of my marriage, I saw very clearly that it was not a road I took by accident. It wasn't because I didn't have a map or someone to lead me. I wasn't a victim of circumstances, and the devil didn't make me do it. And it certainly wasn't God's will, as some claim when they begin an affair. No, I take full responsibility for the road I traveled.

So how in the world did I, a woman who had been raised in the shadow of the church by Christ-centered parents, grandparents, and aunts and uncles; who had married a minister and stood by his side for more than 20 years as we loved and served God's family, end up on the brink of utter ruin in the midst of the whole assembly? (See 5:14.)

There is just one answer. During a prolonged season of discontent when spiritual and marital wells ran dry and love waxed cold, I turned away from the wisdom of God and embraced the wisdom of this world. I ignored God's words, His warnings—His signs—and stepped off the narrow path.

> For the time will come when men will not put up with sound doctrine. Instead, to suit their own desires, they will gather around them a great number of teachers to say what their itching ears want to hear *(2 Tim. 4:3)*.

*It is a lie that God will stop you
if He wants you to stop.*

We cannot say "I didn't know," for God's wisdom beckons from every corner of our lives and leaves us without excuse.

A woman once said to me, "I prayed and prayed that I wouldn't fall into the temptation of adultery, but I did. Why didn't God stop me?" The truth is that she didn't want to be stopped. She knew where moral lines are drawn, but she chose to step over them.

When we blame God, we are saying that He failed to warn us, but His boundaries and warnings are very clear.

Are you dancing around moral boundaries?

Applying Truth

Jesus says in Matt. 7:13, "Enter through the narrow gate. For wide is the gate and broad is the road that leads to destruction, and many enter through it." When it comes to immorality and divorce, the road is wide, not because God has widened it for our convenience but because so many are on it. The wide road to destruction is not the place where Christians and non-Christians should be rubbing elbows—but they are.

- What road are you on?
- If you are on the broad road, where do you expect this road to lead you?
- Where does God say it will take you?
- If you are on the narrow road, what will it take to stay on it?

Read Prov. 1:20-33.

- Whose wisdom are you listening to?
- What is this wisdom saying to you?
- If you are not hearing God's wisdom, why do you think that is?
- What do you need to do to hear God's wisdom?

Is your spiritual or marital well dry? When that

happens, the polluted water the world has to offer begins to look good. My poison was adultery, but there are other wells that offer unclean waters that promise to fill the voids in our lives.

- We escape into our careers.
- We escape into our children, extended family, or friends.
- We escape into alcohol or substance abuse.
- We escape by engaging in private chat rooms or in pornography.
- We escape with steamy romance novels or soap operas.
- We escape through emotional affairs.
- We escape through excessive spending or shopping.
- We escape into church or community work.

With this in mind, hear what Jer. 2:13 says, "My people have committed two sins: They have forsaken me, the spring of living water, and have dug their own cisterns, broken cisterns that cannot hold water." We are thirsty people, and when we do not possess true wisdom, we search apart from the only One whose well of Living Water never runs dry.

- What broken cistern are you escaping to?
- What leaks (spiritual, emotional, relational, physical, financial, etc.) is that broken cistern creating in your life?

Proceed with Caution

*T*oday, we live in a world where the threat of terrorism is real. We are no longer surprised when we awake to hear of terrorist activity and find ourselves under a Red Alert. We realize there could be an attack anywhere in the United States, but for the most part we really don't expect an attack to occur where we live.

Make no mistake, Christian marriages are under attack—everywhere. Consider all that Satan gains when a solid Christian marriage surrenders to his attack. Shock rips through the church, the kingdom of God appears weak and unable to protect its own, and the message of the gospel is crippled.

I grew up in church and became a pastor's wife. One would think that I would have developed a sixth sense that would warn me of danger. But actually, the reverse happened. I became very complacent, thinking that my background and position in ministry had given me a spiritual edge and special protection. I didn't heed the signs all around me that said "Danger Ahead!"

Today, Christian marriages face unparalleled stress and enormous temptations. Satan rejoices when the world receives the message that Christians who proclaim the power of the gospel and the resurrection of Jesus Christ are in marriages that are just as vulnerable as those of the unbelieving world.

At the core of a Christian marriage is the love of God, the promise of redemption and reconciliation that flows from the Cross, and the power to overcome through the resurrection of Jesus Christ. When I gave Satan a foothold and he triumphed in our Christian home, the powerful message that was sent to unbelievers was that the cross of Jesus Christ and the power of His resurrection were powerless to mend and heal what was broken in our lives and in our marriages.

When Christian marriages fail—as mine did—
the watching world says we believed in vain. It says
that the death of Christ, the power of His resurrection,
and the love of God are powerless to thwart sin and to
transform lives and reconcile us to one another.

A study conducted by the George Barna Research
Group tells us "that the likelihood of married adults
getting divorced is identical among born again Christians and those who are not born again."[1]

There is never a day when Christians wake up to a
low-risk, Green Alert day. Satan's terrorist activities
against our marriages are relentless. And it pains me to
know that I was not diligent in protecting my family.

Sometimes I imagine Satan approaching God and
initiating a conversation similar to the one they had
about Job. "Does Lyndell fear God for nothing? . . .
Have you not put a hedge around her and her home,
and all that she has, on every side? But stretch out your
hand and strike everything she has, and she will surely
curse you to your face" (see Job 1:9-11).

Given the events that rolled over our lives in
1998, I can't help but wonder if Satan was given per-
mission to sift me as wheat (see Luke 22:31). All I
know is that I failed miserably. I was not at all Job-like.

*It is a lie that your past spiritual
successes protect you from Satan's
ploys against your marriage.*

To be complacent about Satan's desire to destroy your witness and your very life is one of the first steps on the road to ruin.

Here are some facts that you may not have heard for a long time:

- The existence of Satan is taught in seven Old Testament books and by every New Testament writer.

- Jesus acknowledged and taught the existence of Satan. (Matt. 13:39; Luke 10:18; 11:18 are a few.)

- Satan is the god of this age (2 Cor. 4:4); he is the evil one (1 John 5:19); he is a murderer and a liar (John 8:44); he is a confirmed sinner (1 John 3:8); he is an accuser (Rev. 12:10); he is an adversary (1 Pet. 5:8).

- He appears as a serpent (Rev. 12:9); dragon (v. 3); angel of light (2 Cor. 11:14).

- In relation to Christians, he tempts them to lie (Acts 5:3); he accuses and slanders them (Rev. 12:10); he hinders their work (1 Thess. 2:18); he employs demons to attempt to defeat them (Eph. 6:11-12); he tempts them to immorality (1 Cor. 7:5); he incites persecution against them (Rev. 2:10).

There is good news, though.

- He has no reign in heaven, for he was cast out from his original position (Ezek. 28:16).

- Although he won a victory in Eden, he lost the

battle for eternity, for judgment was pronounced then and there by God (Gen. 3:14-15).

- The cross of Jesus took away Satan's final blow
  —it took away the sting of death (John 12:31).
- The day will come when he will be cast into
  the lake of fire along with his cohorts for all
  eternity to never again tempt humankind (Rev.
  20:10).

Applying Truth

As we wait for the foe to be permanently defeat-
ed, there are things we can do to protect ourselves. Jesus tells us to "watch and pray so that you will not fall
into temptation. The spirit is willing, but the body is
weak" (Mark 14:38).

Our instruction is twofold: watch and pray. First,
we are to watch. A simple command, yet so easily forgotten. Watching requires that we:

- Recognize that Satan is a very real danger and
  we must be alert.
- Study the Scriptures so that we become aware
  of Satan's nature and his tactics.
- Acknowledge that it will take wisdom that we
  do not possess to resist him. The Word of God
  is the weapon that will insure our victory.
- Remember that we are not immune to Satan's
  deception. Someone once said, "Where one
  man can go, any man can go."

In Mark 14:32-38, Jesus asked His disciples to keep watch for one hour. One hour was all He asked for. Not two. Not five. Not all day. Just one hour to watch, to pray, lest we fall into temptation. He knew that if we watch well, we will be supersensitive to what is happening around us—in our lives and in the lives of others. He knew that watching would enhance our awareness of Satan's strategies—his lies, cunning, and deceit.

Jesus was aware of the spiritual battle for our souls. It drove Him to falling on His face in prayer near the slumbering disciples. God's Word tells us that Jesus was tempted like we are—His flesh and His Spirit were at war. His flesh was under attack, for the divine was calling Him to make an incredible sacrifice—death on a cross, for the souls of all creation were at stake. His keen alertness to Satan's power kept Him facedown in prayer until He could finally say, "Yet not my will, but yours be done" (Luke 22:42). No wonder He warned the disciples to keep watching and to keep praying. The temptation to give in to what the flesh desires is strong. Jesus knew how real the struggle is. We must not easily dismiss it.

I wonder what would happen in our lives if we gave one hour to watching and praying. One hour to watch and become keenly aware of Satan's attacks upon our flesh. One hour to acknowledge that in our own strength we can do nothing against Satan. One hour in which we agree with Jesus that we will commit to daily watchfulness and prayer, lest we abandon Him like the disciples did.

If you are engaging in deceitfulness; if you are gratifying the flesh by carrying out its desires; if your marriage is under attack and you are tempted to bail, think back to what your "watch and pray" life was like in the weeks or months before you took such a wrong turn.

How do you get back on track? Wake up. Look around you. Don't allow ruin to be your wake-up call.

- Go back to confession, prayer, and the study of Scripture. Stay on your knees until you can pray like Jesus: "Not my will, but yours be done." Then no matter how difficult, *obey*.

- Write down your commitment, telling God what you will do to get back on track. Can you watch and pray one hour each day? If not, how much? Describe how and when you will fit it into your day.

3

Sharp Curves Ahead

*L*ife is difficult. That became very clear to me in 1998. I discovered that I was poorly prepared for the trials that year brought.

The year began with my father facing open-heart surgery. It was the first time he had faced a serious illness—the first time I had ever seen him in the hospital. It was traumatic for our whole family. A few weeks later, a spot found on my mother's pancreas threw us into a panic in light of her battle with breast cancer a few years earlier. After a battery of tests, the medical experts still didn't know what it was but advised us that it should be watched closely. In February, my brother, with whom I am very close, announced that after 23 years of marriage and three children, his marriage was ending. That decision rocked our circle of family and friends, and I found myself swept up in an all-consuming effort to save his marriage and soothe distraught family members.

While this drama was unfolding, a tragedy occurred that shattered the small town we lived in and hurtled me into deep emotional and spiritual depression. My cousin and his family lived a few doors down from us. On Tuesday morning, August 25, 1998, as my friend and I drove toward my cousin's home, we noticed a small form lying in the middle of the road, a man standing over it. Drawing closer, I realized with horror that the small form was Kirby, five years old, and my cousin's youngest child. The man standing over him was a neighbor who had been driving by when Kirby tripped and fell onto the road in front of his car. As my friend and I began to administer CPR, his frantic mother dialed 911. For more than 20 minutes, my friend and I struggled to revive an unconscious little boy whose broken and twisted body lay between us. The ambulance finally arrived and whisked Kirby away. An hour later, as friends, family, and neighbors gathered in the emergency room, Kirby was pronounced dead—something my friend and I suspected long before the ambulance arrived.

I went home, threw my blood-soaked clothes away, and fell to my knees. The shattered and frantic faces of Kirby's parents, their desperate pleas to my friend and me to not stop CPR, the angelic whiteness of Kirby's face, all closed in on me. I crumpled in a heap before God.

Why, God? This makes no sense to me! How can the death of this precious little boy profit anyone or anything? How can you stand by and allow this to happen? Where are you, God? Where are you?

Other unresolved issues with God resurfaced. The recent death of one of my 11th grade students who had died in a car accident while on the way to a family dinner on Christmas Eve; the freakish death of a childhood friend who stood at my wedding, killed while plowing his field when his tractor flipped over and landed on him, suffocating him; my brother's dying marriage. I railed at God. *Do you not see? Do you not care?* I began to doubt. I doubted God's goodness. I doubted that He cared. I doubted that He could deliver. I doubted that He was even paying attention. I heard nothing but silence.

The road of life I had been cruising on suddenly developed sharp, unexpected curves. Grief has a way of veering us off course, exposing not only our souls but also our entire lives—our faith, our beliefs, and our significant relationships. Grief triggers emotions that may have been dormant for years, and as those emotions resurface they bring with them a host of unresolved feelings and fears.

Every illusion was stripped away, leaving me standing exposed before God. The questions I fired at God, the accusations I leveled at Him, and the walls I built began to reveal to me that I was full of fluff. In *Flame of Love: A Theology of the Holy Spirit,* Clark Pinnock tells us, "The purpose of troubling experiences is to wean us from our idea of a God who always pampers us and to bring us to God as He really is, our rock and fortress."[1] I failed to see that.

Instead of being humble and grateful for the hedge that had been around my life, I had come to *expect* it. Like Job, I was deficient in my knowledge of God. Oswald Chambers wrote, "If you know who God is, you will not care what He does."[2] When my comfortable life disappeared, I demanded answers, revealing not only what I thought of God but also how little I knew Him. No wonder I heard only silence.

Grief stripped away my false illusions about

God, and it began to strip away the illusions surrounding my marriage. Grief began to awaken other
emotions that had been suppressed for years. But just
as quickly as the emotions appeared, I smothered
them. I held no hope that they could be addressed
satisfactorily. I didn't sense freedom from what bound
me; instead, I felt further trapped by God, marriage,
and church. There seemed to be no outlet for my pain
and confusion.

> *It is a lie that God cannot be*
> *found in our sufferings.*

Suffering offers us the opportunity to find that He
does not fit at all into the box we keep Him in. He is
so much bigger!

Applying Truth

In 1998, I was oblivious to this. Instead of humbling myself before Him, I despised and kicked at the
events in my life that might have led me to know Him
more fully. Eventually, my rebellious attitude was
manifested in adultery because I refused to recognize
that it is in our suffering that we are best instructed
about God's true character. As we come to learn who
He really is, we come to trust Him more and more as

life gets increasingly difficult. Our trials always lead us back to one question: *Can I trust Him, even in this?* When our answer is "Maybe not," we are blinded to God's good and active presence in our lives.

Think of the anxieties that plague you right now. Fear, pain, worries, doubts. The events you are facing may be much more traumatic than what I faced years ago, or maybe they are less. Regardless of the level of pain that brings each of us to a breaking point, we must direct our attention to the deeper issue of whether or not God really cares about us. And when we decide that maybe He does not, we decide that maybe we can't trust Him. Maybe He is not dependable.

The Israelites exhibited this line of thinking when their lives became difficult. God said, "They tried Me, though they had seen My work" (Ps. 95:9, NASB). They had seen His miraculous deliverance from Egyptian bondage, the parting of the Red Sea, manna falling from heaven, water gushing from a rock, and a cloud by day and a pillar of fire by night. Still, when they encountered sharp curves, they asked, "Can we trust Him in this?"

What works has God done in your life? Can you name them? Do you call them deliverances or do you call them coincidences? Were they really God's work— evidence that He heard your cry? Are they evidence that He has come through for you in the past? God challenges us to look at His works when we doubt.

Today, as I remember 1998, I can identify God at work in areas where I accused Him of being absent. My rebellious heart had closed my eyes to His presence, my ears to His comforting promises, and my heart to His healing touch. I know now that there is nothing so ugly or painful that it could cause God to abandon us. A loving and wise God is here to stay, and He is in control. He wants our unflinching trust. "He wants us to look at the darkest, blackest fact full in the face without damaging His character. Until we can do that, we do not know Him."[3]

- Look back over your life. Look at the good times as well as the bad times. What evidence can you point to that reveals that God is here to stay and will not leave you?

- Have you looked into the past and into your present and still not seen evidence of God working on your behalf? Then look up. The greatest work God has done for you is the cross of Jesus Christ. In light of this wondrous work, let us not test God with unbelief.

- Are there areas in your life where you are testing God due to unbelief? If so, confess them to God, and pray—every day if you must—*Lord, I believe, help thou mine unbelief* (Mark 9:24, KJV).

The Road of Turmoil and Confusion

*D*uring the turbulence that overtook my life in 1998, the problems in my marriage could no longer be denied. I was in my 40s, had been married for 25 years, and the dissatisfaction and unhappiness I had managed to silence for years began to find a strong voice.

With so much stress in my life, I desperately needed the haven of comfort and safety that marriage was supposed to offer. But when I attempted to turn to my marriage for comfort and strength, I found it empty. We had invested so little in our marriage relationship that when I needed it most, it had nothing to give.

I vividly remember standing at dusk at my kitchen sink, my hands busy in soapy water, tears streaming down my face. *Face it, Lyndell. This is your marriage. It is nothing like you thought it would be. You're stuck, trapped, for the rest of your life.* Outrage and despair churned in my soul toward the lonely and bleak future that yawned before me. But I squared my shoulders and accepted my "cross," or so I thought at the time. The truth is, those feelings went underground— unconfessed and unutterable—before a silent God. Buried there, they went to work building strongholds of disillusionment and bitterness, and a stream of rebellion began to carve its way through my soul.

During that tumultuous year, David had taken a job with a different company. Having always loved the world of finance and helping people manage their money, he had resigned from the pastorate in 1996 and taken a job with a financial company that allowed him to do what fascinated him. In 1998, he changed companies and, because it tripled his territory, it was a stressful time, taking months to get established. In the meantime, our income was cut in half, and it required long hours each day and sometimes nights away from home.

We were the typical American family—ships passing in the night. We still had two teenagers at home going in several different directions. David was on the road, and with continued church and community involvement and extended family demands, we lived on the edge of frenzy all the time. As I look back on this season of our lives, I realize that much of the anxiety and restlessness I experienced was because our values and behavior were miles apart. I claimed with my mouth that I valued God, marriage, and family, but my frantic behavior told a different story. I have discovered that there can be no peace when that which we deeply value is not deeply lived. It is very difficult to slow down—even on the sharp curves—when you're used to speeding. Thus, instead of feeling intimacy and comfort from the people I valued most, I felt estranged and restless.

That same year, our third child left for college, with our fourth and youngest not far behind. As I faced the dwindling nest, realizing that except for me it might as well be empty, I panicked. If little has been invested in the marriage—with children or anything else coming first—when the nest empties, we ask ourselves, "Who is this strange bird in my nest?"

I felt trapped. I found no solace in my marriage or in my relationship with God. I had been deficient in my knowledge of God and asleep to Satan's cunning schemes. Charles Spurgeon describes this process well:

> Satan shows his cunning by the times in which he attacks us . . . he therefore comes upon us when there is a cloud between ourselves and God. When the body is depressed and the spirits are weak, then he will tempt us and try to lead us to distrust God.[1]

Disillusioned with my marriage and feeling betrayed by God, my soul was slowly poisoned, isolating me from my husband and from God. This aching disappointment began to manifest itself in bitterness and rebellion.

It wasn't long before I felt isolated from the community of believers. Although I didn't *act* isolated, I was isolated inwardly by shame and defeat that plagued me constantly. The result was a deeply ingrained belief that there was no safe space with God or His people where I could confess my feelings without being rejected. I was surrounded by Christians, but I felt alone and trapped. This isolation was the result of early church teaching that said it was wrong for Christians to struggle with the temptations of life, and if they did, there was something lacking in their faith. I had been taught that disillusionment, discouragement, temptation, and depression were all symptoms of a life that was either unredeemed or unsanctified. A good Christian would never admit dissatisfaction with his or her marriage—especially a ministry couple. And never would a Christian express disappointment with God. Wasn't that akin to blasphemy? Since these feelings were not allowed to exist in the first place, I never felt the freedom to express or confess them to God or anyone else.

My adulthood was shaped by these beliefs, as were my marriage and ministry. Driven by this paradigm, I felt that I could never measure up, that God loved only those who had their acts together, and that He sat in judgment of me. So I worked very hard at projecting the image of one who *did* have her act together. I became the perfect pastor's wife; I was a tower of spiritual strength. I was a person with a smile and an answer for every trial or temptation. A sin such as adultery was dismissed as something I was incapable of. I was, after all, above that kind of sin.

Naturally, this behavior placed me on a pedestal where others knew they could always find me—high on wisdom, strength, and victory. This proved to be a lonely place to be and an impossible place to stay. Hiding feelings that brought shame and embarrassment created tension between my "perfect" life and my heart, which was anything but perfect. Divorce was not an option; and because I had an image to protect, neither was counseling.

The swelling tide of misery over my lot in life— particularly with my marriage—would soon knock me off my lofty perch before God and His people. Having no confidence in my marriage, God, or my church as places I could confess my unhappiness, led to avoidance and further isolation and to considering a road that held the promise of bypassing all of my concerns.

It is a lie that you can simply hop on another road to detour around a difficult road and find the peace and joy you yearn for.

Gordon MacDonald wrote in *A Resilient Life,* "I believe the forties to be dangerous, uncharted waters for a lot of us. . . . There are new questions that pop up in one's forties. Lots of things begin to happen for which many of us are unprepared."[2] When problems occur for which we have no answers, we feel trapped and isolated. We are supposed to be grown up by our 40s, aren't we? We're supposed to have solid answers for ourselves and for others. But I wanted to avoid that road full of questions without answers that left me on shaky ground. My old answers no longer fit these new questions. And because the knowledge I had gained about how to function as a Christian adult was erroneous and false, I naturally came up with a wrong way to cope.

Applying Truth

Many Christians shy away from *doctrine,* as I did at one time, but doctrine is what Christians believe and what they practice. *Right beliefs* we hold about God and His love, about salvation, about Christianity, about Scripture, about death and life, about eternity, are what undergird our faith in the midst of suffering. *Wrong beliefs* undermine our faith. Unexpected curves on the road of life can sorely test our beliefs. If our beliefs are twisted and warped, then the answers we find will not be healthy and will lead only to chaos and confusion.

As I have reexamined my journey, God has revealed to me three types of ignorance that I was guilty of that influenced my beliefs and my behavior. We will discuss two of the types of ignorance here: naive ignorance and blind ignorance.

Naive ignorance is believing that what we understood from our childhood faith will be adequate to meet the challenges of adulthood. My first mistake was to believe that my marriage, my church, and my Christian friends were all I needed to meet and satisfy my deepest needs. If you are putting your faith in anyone or anything other than God, you are guaranteed to end up disillusioned. Yet it happens—a lot.

Christians drive to church thinking it is there they will find the one and only source of peace and joy. The church is not responsible for your growth into a mature knowledge of God. Only you and God can achieve that.

Another mistake was the perception I had that good Christians do not face temptation, discouragement, or unhappiness. But with God's wisdom all around us in the Bible, prayer, and other good Christian literature, we will not be let off the hook when it comes to accountability. Even when life's curves threaten to stop us in our tracks, we remain childishly naive about the huge gaps in our knowledge of God and ourselves. Like the woman Folly in Prov. 9:13, we are undisciplined and without knowledge.

Blind ignorance happens when our disillusionment reveals long-denied emotions and, instead of facing them, we push them down and build new illusions in order to escape our painful reality. We tend to do that because "with much wisdom comes much sorrow; the more knowledge, the more grief" (Eccles. 1:18). The pain and grief that accompany enlightenment of our inner turmoil and outer reality can be overwhelming, but to remain blind to our problems is to never hear God's answers. His answers are tailor-made to target the naive ignorance we have about ourselves and about God and His character.

When Paul faced the thorn in his flesh, he was told three times it would remain and "my grace is sufficient for you" (2 Cor. 12:9). This answer provided him with a knowledge of God he never would have gained had the thorn been removed. It also gave him knowledge about himself and where he stood in relation to God. Would he still trust God, even though God did not remove the thorn? Apparently, Paul's answer was yes. Thus, Paul came to know that hidden within life's difficulties—which are clearly bad—is God's good grace. To deny the harsh realities of life is to deny God the opportunity to reveal depths of His character that we are ignorant of and to mature our faith.

The church we attend, our parents, and other people do not often encourage us to take a deep look inside ourselves. In fact, they often aid us in maintaining illusions, because to look deeply at ourselves can be scary and messy and leave those who care about us wondering how to contain the can of worms that has been opened.

We cannot use the limitations of others, though, as an excuse to stay in our ignorance about what is going on inside of us and about who God is and how He wants to address our issues. Don't just *carry on* as many Christians do—showing up at church with serene smiles while dying on the inside. To do so is to profess a wisdom we do not possess. "Although they claimed to be wise, they became fools" (Rom. 1:22).

Eventually, someone will call your bluff—most likely God—and you will fall from your lofty perch and land facedown in the dust. You will shift blame and point your finger at your church, your spouse, and God, when all the while it was your own ignorance that betrayed you.

Ask yourself the following questions as they pertain to marriage, your family, your church, and God:

- What naive ignorance am I holding onto in each of these areas of my life? What beliefs have I carried over from childhood that are no longer adequate for the adult challenges I face?
- What blind ignorance do I engage in concerning these four areas? Are there troubling issues that keep surfacing that I refuse to address?

5

The Detour to Rebellion

Detours always take longer in the long run, and they're usually rougher and harder to travel than the original road. But when our lives seem impossible, it's easy to be lured to a detour as a way around our painful realities. We are warned in James 1:14 (NASB): "But each one is tempted when he is carried away and enticed by his own lust." Temptation is strongest when we long to be carried away from our difficult circumstances and our crumbled illusions that reveal the ugly realities of life.

It is at this place in our lives we are most vulnerable to Satan's offer of another way out. Having allowed life to pull the Rock out from under my feet, I found myself disillusioned with my marriage, with God, and with other believers. I was left with no outlet. I said to myself, "I *tried* God and Christianity. I *tried* to make my marriage work. I *tried* to find solace within the church." I felt I was left with nothing. I believed there was nothing else to do.

When we Christians find ourselves thus trapped, isolation, frightening emotions, and mass confusion redefine us. When the door is closed to the life we thought we would have—closed to our spouse because of the hard heart we have developed, closed to God's people because we fear they will reject us, closed to God because we believe that His love is conditional and we have failed to earn it—when meltdown is occurring in every significant area of our lives, to what or to whom we open the door to find comfort makes all the difference.

There is no way to overstate the need for caution, for it is out of these chaotic, hidden emotions that lustful desires are conceived that can give birth to sin. (See James 1:15.) And 1 Peter further reminds us that waiting right outside the door of our confusion is a roaring lion "looking for someone to devour."

Remember this: *When a lion closes in for the kill of a helpless prey, all the hard work has been done. He has isolat-*

ed his prey from the pack and chased it down until weari-
ness and fatigue has it swaying on its feet. He has pursued it
over strange and rocky terrain and it is now lost, confused,
and frightened. Perfect conditions now exist for an easy kill.
Before the victim can take one more step, before it can utter
a cry for help, the lion leaps and has it in its powerful grip.
There is no escape, no way out. Death is imminent.

Christians do not just wake up one morning and decide to exchange the wisdom of God for Satan's lies. Not at all. It is, rather, a slow melting of one's faith—and Satan stalks his prey to the end. Notice the conditions that lead us to drop our faith like crumbs, little by little, on the road to ruin:

- We find ourselves trapped in our circumstances and hemmed in by confusion.
- Life has pushed and pursued us over rocky and unfamiliar terrain until we are weary in doing good.
- Unresolved, taboo emotions have paralyzed us with fear.
- Our struggles have isolated us from God's people.
- We feel abandoned by God and His goodness.

When I found myself cornered by disillusionment with life and marriage, unresolved and forbidden emotions, and a false belief that God and His people sat in judgment of me, I was deceived into believing that since I had already crossed the line by harboring taboo emotions, I might as well cross the line with my actions. Thus, it wasn't long before the troubling and negative emotions that surrounded the two most important relationships in my life—God and marriage—had me convinced that I had already sinned; I had already crossed the line. I felt God had turned His face from me. When presented with the detour of adultery, my rebellious attitude answered, "Why not?"

If I could boil my disobedience down to a simple formula, it would be this: *If you allow hard and bitter issues to fester long in the heart, it will lead to a hardened, rebellious heart, which will lead to rebellious living and a hard life.*

Adultery is a hard life, a hard road. To choose its way is a hardhearted response to the world in which we live. Having allowed the hard realities of my world to back me into a corner, I came out fighting it by joining it—through adultery.

When I began an affair, it was not a road I took by accident. I had packed my bags and I was deliberately running away from home. Certainly, I had come down a long and winding road to get to this place, for I was not one who would have suddenly decided to have an affair. It was the culmination of naive and blind ignorance about God and life, a lax attitude toward Satan's agenda, and wrong beliefs that led to wrong conclusions that led to a slow melting of my faith. Having arrived at this detour, void of real knowledge and wisdom, I unwittingly left room for warped wisdom and knowledge to move in. Only a warped heart without real wisdom can hear God's warnings as found in Isaiah and still take a detour:

> Therefore hear this now, you who are given to pleasures, who dwell securely, who say in your heart, "I am, and there is no one else besides me; I shall not sit as a widow, nor shall I know the loss of children"; but these two things shall come to you in a moment, in one day: the loss of children, and widowhood. They shall come upon you in their fullness because of the multitude of your sorceries, for the great abundance of your enchantments. For you have trusted in your wickedness; you have said, "No one sees me"; your wisdom and your knowledge have warped you; and you have said in your heart, "I am, and there is no one else besides me" (47:8-10, NKJV).

I clearly remember my thinking and how I rationalized my affair: *God obviously does not see or care about what is happening in my life; I am sure He won't see or care about this either.* To commit such gross sin, our warped minds and hearts lead us to believe that no one sees me; God does not see me; therefore, "*I am, and there is no one else besides me.*" Given my spiritual decline, it is no wonder—and it still brings me shame to admit it—that a fist rose up in my heart and I shook it at God as I toppled over the edge into adultery.

It is a lie that the struggle lies
between a husband and wife.

The real struggle is between each spouse and God. There is not one thing you and I face within our marriages that is not ultimately between us and God.

Applying Truth

In the previous chapter, I alluded to three types of ignorance that influenced my beliefs and behavior. The first two were naive ignorance and blind ignorance. Now we'll discuss the third: willful ignorance.

Willful ignorance occurs when naive ignorance and blind ignorance are not met head-on, acknowledged, and addressed. The Israelites are an example of willful ignorance. Lack of knowledge and understanding on the part of the Israelites often led them to rebel against God with acts of stupidity. Worshiping wood idols was one. It led to God mocking their behavior: "No one recalls, nor is there knowledge and understanding to say, 'I have burned half of it in the fire and also have baked bread over its coals. I roast meat and eat it. Then I make the rest of it into an abomination,

I fall down before a block of wood!'" (44:19, NASB).
Their willfulness led them to blockhead behavior, but
before we point fingers, consider how easily we today
turn to gods of our own making:

> For since the creation of the world His invisi-
> ble attributes, His eternal power and divine na-
> ture, have been clearly seen, being understood
> through what has been made, so that they are
> without excuse. For even though they knew God,
> they did not honor Him as God or give thanks,
> but they became futile in their speculations, and
> their foolish heart was darkened. Professing to be
> wise, they became fools. . . . Therefore God gave
> them over in the lusts of their hearts to impurity,
> so that their bodies would be dishonored among
> them. For they exchanged the truth of God for a
> lie, and worshipped and served the creature rather
> than the Creator *(Rom. 1:20-22, 24-25, NASB)*.

Adultery is a prime example of how we worship and
serve the creature rather than the Creator. Immorality is
the idolatry of our age, making us no different from the
Israelites who bowed down before a block of wood. To
remain in such ignorance is to end up on a slippery
slope that leads to folly and destruction, "My people
are destroyed from lack of knowledge" (Hos. 4:6).

Willful disobedience manifested by adultery was
where my naive and blind ignorance led me, and I was
without excuse. Yet I had the audacity, in my ignorance,

to shake my fist at God and smear His character. I knew Him, but I did not honor Him. I engaged in foolish speculations that only further darkened my heart. Like Job, I cast doubt upon God's counsel. I spoke without knowledge, and my words were without wisdom. (See Job 34:35.) My rebellion, like Job's, was a reaction to what I perceived an unjust God had done. I now believe that behind all the ignorant behavior of humanity is first a problem between us and God.

- Before we become disillusioned with life, we are disillusioned with God.
- Before we are cold and aloof in our marriage, we are cold and aloof with God.
- Before we commit adultery, we commit idolatry against God.

Ultimately, I had to answer these core questions concerning my life and my relationship with God:

- Who is going to be in charge of my life—me or God?
- Will I conduct my life according to the world's wisdom or God's Word?
- Will I trust in a false god (the creature) or the true and living Creator God?

Eventually, God's wisdom led me to understand these things:

- The redemption of my marriage would begin with the redemption of me.

- Reconciliation with my spouse would begin with reconciliation between God and me.
- Rebuilding my marriage would begin with the rebuilding of God's wisdom in me.

Ask yourself whether you are being willfully ignorant in your marriage, your relationship with your family, your relationship with your church, or your relationship with God.

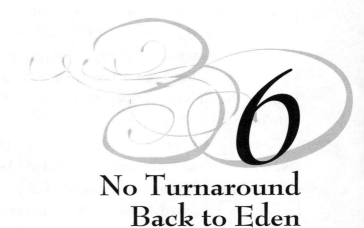

No Turnaround
Back to Eden

*H*ow can Christians, knowing what we know about God, rebel and enter into blatant sin? We know that He is watching. We know that He is listening. We know that He is deeply grieved. In order to turn away from Him, we must first build a case *against* Him. In addition to being deceived into believing He no longer sees or cares, we must also believe that He has become the foe and stands in the way of happiness.

Satan first led Eve to believe that God was no longer her friend but her foe. In order to do that, he created suspicion about God's fairness and goodness. He's still doing that today; he feeds us lies when we are enticed by something we know God has placed off-limits. *Why would a good God withhold something that's good for me? Why would a good God withhold something that would make me happy? Why would a good God withhold something that would fulfill my desires?*

The message has not changed through the ages. *God is unfair. God is not good. God cannot be trusted.* That was the message whispered in my ear as 1998 unfolded.

I had been a Christian all my life. Yet I decided to take my life into my own hands. I decided to take charge of my own happiness. I decided to take what I had decided I deserved. It was time to do things *my* way.

The world's wisdom had my ear. *I have a right to decide what's good for me. I have a right to happiness. I have desires that need to be met. I can't make others happy if I'm not happy. Why would a good God withhold that which feels so right?* I exchanged the wisdom of God for the wisdom of the world, and it was all about me.

The "all about me" approach to life lives for today and gives no thought to tomorrow. A. W. Tozer wrote:

> Sin is always an act of wrong judgment. To commit a sin a man [or woman] must for the

moment believe that things are different from what they really are; he must confound values; he must accept a lie as truth and see truth as a lie; he must ignore the signs on the highway and drive with his eyes shut; he must act as if he has no soul and was not accountable for his moral choices. . . . Sin sees only today, never next month or next year. Death and judgment are pushed aside as if they did not exist and the sinner becomes for the time a practical atheist who by his act denies not only the existence of God but the concept of life and death.[1]

Tozer's words paint a picture of what *no turnaround* looks like. We may bend the rules a little bit, but we would like to think that we are strong enough to avoid reaching a place of no turnaround. We tell ourselves that we could never become so selfish that our lives would become "all about me." But somewhere along the road, we find ourselves swept away to a place of no return, and we cannot identify exactly where the tide turned.

Caught in this swelling tide, we become so victimized and so justified that we rationalize with ease the lies that are blinding us to God's wisdom. At the very heart of our thinking are the strongholds of self-centeredness, pride, and rebellion.

If you are swept away in this tide, soon you will be wallowing in self-pity, seeing that things are in a pitiful state, and living in the pit. It is very difficult to turn around a life that has become "all about me." Eventually, your body will follow where your heart and mind already are: the pit.

Eve reached out and took the fruit because she was convinced it would really bring her life, not death. She believed she was right and God was wrong. When we take the road to adultery, we are convinced that God no longer knows what is best for us and that a new relationship will bring life to our deathlike existence. Little do we realize that "many are the victims she [adultery] has brought down; her slain are a mighty throng. Her house is a highway to the grave, leading down to the chambers of death" (Prov. 7:26-27).

It is a lie that a road that leads us away from God is a road to freedom.

In the final analysis, our will either leads us toward God or away from Him. We cannot have our way and God's way simultaneously, though we often try.

Until we nail down that our will is surrendered to God in obedience because we are the creatures and He is the Creator, our will is up for grabs. To allow our will to be mastered by the flesh is to be in danger of reaching a point of no return. John Wesley said:

> We are shaped . . . in wickedness, conceived
> in sin. Our nature is altogether corrupt in every
> power and faculty. Our will, equally depraved
> with the rest, is wholly bent to indulge our natu-
> ral corruption. . . . By following our own will in
> anything, we strengthen the perverseness of it. By
> indulging it, we continually increase the corrup-
> tion of our nature.[2]

Romans 1:24 shows this picture, "Therefore God gave them over in the sinful desires of their hearts to sexual impurity for the degrading of their bodies with one another."

Does God really abandon us in this instance? I believe He does, in the sense that when God *gave them over*, He gave them over to their own rule—to their own lusts, passions, and way of thinking. When we insist on following our own will, He will abandon us to our own wisdom, to our own guidance, and to our own folly. God is still loving us with a tough love when He abandons us like this. His judgment of abandonment is a prelude to our redemption. When we find ourselves in circumstances from which we cannot save ourselves, we will cry out to Him. For some of us, it means we must reach the end of our road to ruin. When we choose to make it "all about me," God is grieved, but His hands are tied. He will not violate free will.

He will weep over us as He did Jerusalem:

> If you, even you, had only known on this
> day what would bring you peace—but now it is
> hidden from your eyes. The days will come upon
> you when your enemies will build an embank-
> ment against you and encircle you and hem you
> in on every side. They will dash you to the
> ground *(Luke 19:42-44)*.

Being hemmed in on every side and dashed to the
ground can mean only one thing—captivity.

We serve a jealous God. He will not tolerate a divided allegiance. He will either be Lord of our lives
and Master of our will, or He will abandon us to our
pitiful selves as He watches and weeps.

Some time ago, I had the opportunity to try to
steer a woman away from her rebellious path of adultery. We'll call her Susan. Susan had been married 18
years and was involved in an adulterous affair with a
man who was also married. She said she had found
the love of her life. She had two teenagers and a husband who were begging her to come home. I shared
my story, shared scripture, and shared the certain and
tragic results of a life turned in on itself. Susan, who
professed to be a Christian, was angry at God, at her
husband, and at her mother who had also left home
for another man when Susan was a teenager. She listened to what I said, but with a closed mind and a fist
in her heart. Two months later she filed for divorce.

Applying Truth

A will that refuses to surrender will eventually result in rebellious living. Heed C. S. Lewis's words:

> Fallen man is not simply an imperfect creature who needs improvement: he is a rebel who must lay down his arms. Laying down your arms, surrendering, saying you are sorry, realizing that you have been on the wrong track and getting ready to start life over again from the ground floor—that is the only way out of our "hole." This process of surrender . . . is what Christians call repentance.[3]

Rebellion can be forgiven, but the consequences are forever. The lay of the land and its people are never the same after a rebel army takes over, thus it is with our lives.

It is never too late, however, to lay down your arms—to lay down your will—and surrender to God. If you do, you will hear the words God spoke to me the day I laid down my arms: "Speak comfort to Jerusalem [I put my name here], and cry out to her, that her warfare is ended, that her iniquity is pardoned; for she has received from the LORD's hand double for all her sins" (Isa. 40:2, NKJV).

Though there was ruin all around me, God had forgiven my rebellion. The day I surrendered my will to God, a white flag was raised, and God and I were finally at peace. Only then could the rebuilding process begin on the ruins my warfare had created.

- Have you surrendered your will to God? If you have not, you will have difficulty hearing and obeying God, because your allegiance is divided. When you surrender, you declare to God that He is in charge of your life and that the rebel now submits to a new ruler. If you have not surrendered, what is holding you back?

- What adjustments—mentally, morally, sexually, and relationally—would you need to make if you allowed God to be the sole ruler in your life?

Accident Ahead

*N*early every day we hear of a teenaged driver who has been injured or killed because of speeding. Why do you suppose teenagers continue to speed—even in light of the warnings of adults and when confronted by the death of friends? It's because they believe they are invincible—that death happens to others but never to them. They believe they can beat the odds.

Christians embarking on adultery are much like teenagers behind the wheel. We think we will be the exception. We think we can break God's commands and not become broken ourselves. We believe we can outsmart the lion that seeks to devour us. But God's Word warns that death is definitely—*not maybe*—waiting.

Hear what Prov. 1:31-32 says about taking fruit that is forbidden, "They will eat the fruit of their ways and be filled with the fruit of their schemes. For the waywardness of the simple will kill them, and the complacency of fools will destroy them."

Do you feel that you are trapped in your relationships with no way out except for a detour you know is wrong? Do you feel that God is no longer your friend but your foe? If so, you are very vulnerable to the final blow.

The final blow is summed up like this, "Then, after desire has conceived, it gives birth to sin; and sin, when it is full-grown, gives birth to death" (James 1:15). James says that not life, but death, is birthed.

It is a lie that adultery will give you a second chance at love and happiness and new hope for a happier future.

At some point for all of us, life becomes hard. Marriages disappoint. Children challenge. Loved ones die. God seems silent. Without much warning, we suddenly feel that life is running over us, leaving us vulnerable. Instead of turning to God, the One who sees, knows, cares, and possesses power, we Christians are turning away in droves to other gods. We are like the Israelites who demanded of Aaron, "Make us gods who will go before us. As for this fellow Moses who led us out of Egypt—we don't know what has happened to him!" (Acts 7:40).

When we fear that God has abandoned us and that He doesn't care or that He is silent or powerless, we are vulnerable to following another god. What or who is your other god? Who are you expecting to rescue you from the hardships of life, from deep loneliness in your marriage, from aching disappointment with God? When the wellspring of my faith evaporated, Satan's polluted well offered me another god—adultery.

A few days after my affair was discovered, bringing me face-to-face with the reality of what I had done, I wrote these words in my journal:

If I could just go back—just go back and undo all I have done, I would, in a heartbeat. I have wept for days on end. I have experienced more pain than I have ever felt, caused more pain than I thought myself capable of. My foolishness robbed me of the woman I used to be. I used to be a good person; a good woman in the sense that I had integrity; a clear sense of right and wrong; I could

disdain perversity. I recognized sin and could be re-
pulsed by its darkness. Yet I have done the unthink-
able. I turned to the god of adultery, thinking I
could find love, happiness, and comfort in the arms
of stolen pleasure. Instead, it comforted in vain, for
it has proven to be a bitter, bitter curse! It was not
a savior! The god who I thought would carry me,
conned me instead. It became a cruel master,
chaining me to a prison from which I could not es-
cape. The unhappiness in my life that I had been
trying to escape when I engaged in infidelity was
nothing compared to the bondage and imprison-
ment this god brought to my life and soul!

If only we could see the consequences of our rebellion, I believe that very few of us would stray from
the wisdom of God. To turn from God's wisdom is to
invite calamity into our lives. It is to echo the cry in
Prov. 5:12-14, "How I hate discipline! How my heart
spurned correction! I would not obey my teachers or
listen to my instructors. I have come to the brink of
utter ruin in the midst of the whole assembly."

I was indeed on the verge of ruin in the midst of
the assembly and congregation. Put simply, when I
was on dangerous ground, entertaining a decision
that would place me on the edge of ruin, there were
spiritual flags all around me, saying, "Stop! Listen!
Obey!" If we don't heed those warnings, make no
mistake, destruction waits for us.

If we do stop, listen, and obey, we will discover the way out and the way through. Granted, it is not our way. Like the prodigal son, if you want to turn around and go home again, as I did, there is only one way to be delivered from the hole where your sin has left you.

Even today, I cannot read my journal entry without tears coming to my eyes and my heart feeling gripped with dread. I ask myself, *Who was that woman?* I wonder if it is similar to what King David felt when the prophet Nathan confronted him about his unrepentant heart. Using a parable, Nathan led David to condemn another while a huge plank still remained in his own eye—the sins of adultery and murder. In doing so, he held the mirror to David's face, revealing his sins, and in essence said, "Take a hard look . . . the man you condemn? You are the man!" (See 2 Sam. 12:1-7, NASB.)

There is a difference between saying "I committed adultery" and "I am an adulterer." One places the focus outwardly—at the act and its consequences. The other forces me to look inward—at my own character. David had committed outward acts of sin, but it wasn't until he was confronted with "You are the man" that he realized how far he had fallen from being a man after God's own heart. It was at that moment that he recognized his need to repent and seek forgiveness not only for what he had done but, more importantly, for

what he had become. In his anguish, David pens his
own "journal" entry and cries out to the Lord:

> There is no soundness in my flesh because
> of Your anger, nor any health in my bones be-
> cause of my sin. For my iniquities have gone over
> my head; like a heavy burden they are too heavy
> for me. My wounds are foul and festering be-
> cause of my foolishness. I am troubled, I am
> bowed down greatly. . . . I am feeble and severely
> broken; I groan because of the turmoil of my
> heart. . . . My heart pants, my strength fails me;
> as for the light of my eyes, it also has gone from
> me. My loved ones and my friends stand aloof
> from my plague, and my relatives stand afar off.
> . . . my sorrow is continually before me. For I will
> declare my iniquity; I will be in anguish over my
> sin *(Ps. 38:3-6, 8, 10-11, 17-18, NASB)*.

This is a picture of what sin does to us, both spiritually and physically. It is the picture I see of myself
each time I read my journal. It is the reason I still
weep; it is a reminder of how far I had fallen. It is a reminder of what I had become—an adulterous
woman. It is a reminder of what sin did to me—and
will do to all held in its grip.

We end up in this anguish because we fail to anticipate where that first step over the line will take us.
And it is much further than we wanted or intended to
go. Once sin traps us, it makes all other entrapments

we whined about—marriage, church, God—pale in comparison. The journey of sin and its cost has not changed since it began in Eden with the first family, on to King David, and down to us. What makes us think we will be the exception?

Sin is Satan's business, but restoring brokenness and breaking bondage is God's business. Are you willing to hold the mirror to your face and see if you are in need of repentance and forgiveness? Where are you in this picture of sin?

- Maybe you're not in the picture at all. Maybe you're walking in obedience to God, thankful for His grace that is keeping you.
- Maybe you are at the beginning of sin's journey, harboring deceitful and lustful thoughts and being tempted to cross the line.
- Are you ensnared in sin's cords, unable to break the hold it has over you?
- Are you at the end of sin's journey, broken by the ruin you see around you?

Wherever you are, take a few minutes and write your own journal entry—or psalms—that expresses your emotions and feelings.

In Ps. 38:21-22 (NASB) David writes, "Do not forsake me, O LORD; O my God, do not be far from me! Make haste to help me, O Lord, my salvation!" How will your psalm conclude?

8

Only One Way Back Home

*W*hen I was growing up, I repeatedly heard the message that Jesus is the answer to our every need. I remember joining in with the youth group when I was a teen, jabbing my right index finger to the sky and testifying that Jesus was the One Way—the only way. As a young adult, I knew this in my head—but my heart had yet to experience it. I became a Christian and avoided sin because of my fear of hell more than because of my love for God. I did all the right things for all the wrong reasons. Jesus was my fire insurance. Somehow, that was not very comforting, for the protection was granted from the very One who threatened the flames.

When I was little, I often sat alongside my grandmother on her piano bench as we sang her favorite hymns. I remember one day, as we were singing the chorus to "Victory in Jesus," she stopped abruptly after the words, "He sought me and bought me." With a smile, she asked, "What did you just sing?" As she played the notes again, I sang, "He socked me and bopped me with His redeeming love." She leaned back on her piano bench and laughed till she cried. To this day, when I sing or hear that song, I see her face and hear her laughter. I remember my astonishment that I had missed the actual lyrics. Sometimes I wonder if maybe it was not so much a mistake as a subconscious belief that He was a God who existed to sock me and bop me when I stepped out of line.

I had been exposed to a steady diet of God's wrath toward my sins, the imminent Rapture, and a mental list of what I should and should not do if I wanted to make it to heaven. We were urgently pressed to confess our sins before leaving church because of the possibility of dying in a car accident on the way home. Countless times that warning drove me to the altar, fearing the socking, bopping God who would hold my emotions and my failures against me. I would leave the altar having vowed to try harder, guilty over my lack of love for this angry, judgmental God and afraid I would die and miss heaven.

Fear and false guilt followed me to college. I was

gripped by them when, for the first time in my life at age 18, I sat in a theater to watch *Gone with the Wind*. Movies were forbidden, and I could not enjoy the movie because I expected the Rapture to occur at any moment, and I would spend eternity in hell. I did draw some comfort, however, from the fact that the son of the president of the Christian college I attended was sitting right behind me.

When I became a young adult and then a pastor's wife, fear was my main motivation for serving God. I worked hard to polish my performance, conforming to everyone and everything that smacked of religion in order to perfect the outward marks of Christianity. Inside I was lifeless, joyless, and faithless, because God's love for me had always been suspect. I had religion based upon performance, but I lacked a relationship with God based upon real truth.

The religion I had was cold and compassionless. It beat me with laws I could not keep and then abandoned me when I needed it most. Over the years, religion and God melded into one. After I committed adultery, it was revealed to me that adultery was not my real struggle; the real struggle had always been between me and God.

The day my husband, David, packed up and drove away—taking 25 years of history with him to another state—I walked into my kitchen and could go no further. My knees buckled, I fell to the floor, and let out a wail of despair. Holding my head in my hands, I wept in anguish and disbelief. Five months had passed since my affair was discovered, and we had tried to salvage our marriage. But it all came down to this—me wailing like a madwoman on the kitchen floor and David driving like a madman to get as far away from me as possible.

> *It is a lie that you will find peace in going through the motions of rule-based religion.*

That day on the kitchen floor, the fist I had shaken at God was raised toward Him, groping for His mercy. Suddenly, the God who I thought did not notice or care appeared.

Applying Truth

He will surely be gracious to you at the sound of your cry; when He hears it, He will answer you. Although the Lord has given you bread of privation and water of oppression, He, your Teacher will no longer hide Himself, but your eyes will behold your Teacher *(Isa. 30:19-20, NASB)*.

As the days turned into weeks and months, I looked back on that day as the day my Teacher came out of hiding, and my pride—cloaked in filthy rags of self-righteousness—was revealed. I saw the truth: the consequences I faced were just what I deserved. My rebellion melted, and I was left with these words of King David, "For I know my transgressions, and my sin is always before me. Against you, you only, have I sinned and done what is evil in your sight" (Ps. 51:3-4). In the ruin that surrounded me, my Teacher had spoken, and I found Him just; He had judged, and I found Him blameless.

On my floor I saw and addressed my sin of pride. It was a humbling truth to admit that I truly *do* need a Savior. My outward marks of Christianity, my learned coping strategies, and the life experiences I drew from were not enough to save me. My life was in shambles, and my best thinking had gotten me there. But out of God's great mercy, the justice that was delivered was a prelude to His redeeming love. God had exercised tough love—He had abandoned me to my pitiful self, allowing me to sink into circumstances from which I could not save myself, and I cried out for my Savior.

God still had quite a challenge on His hands, however, as I struggled to receive His forgiveness. In my eyes, adultery was the epitome of sin. It was a sin that I harshly judged in others. It was one of those "I would never do that" sins. Satan's accusations underscored my belief that God had written me off.

But I longed to know and experience the truth of

God's love and forgiveness, for I realized just how bar-ren my life was without it. But the closer I got to mak-ing this truth mine, the case I had built against God's love would rise up and tenaciously grip my heart and mind. I was still wary of God, still seeing Him as judg-mental, unforgiving, and angry, and a God who grudgingly gave His love only after I proved worthy of it. My heart—shriveled from a cold, loveless religion —was incapable of embracing an intimate God who loved me—regardless of my rebellion and sin.

Dear God, I need to know that you love me. I need to know that I am truly forgiven. Deliver me from fears that destroy, from unbelief that alienates me from you.

Desperate, I picked up my Bible and opened it at random. My eyes fell on of Ps. 103:10-13:

> He does not treat us as our sins deserve or repay us according to our iniquities. For as high as the heavens are above the earth, so great is his love for those who fear him; as far as the east is from the west, so far has he removed our trans-gressions from us. As a father has compassion on his children, so the LORD has compassion on those who fear him.

As this truth flooded my soul and began washing away darkness and unbelief, I heard Him tenderly say, "I have never dealt with you according to your sins, for it was I who was severely dealt with in your place. I have not punished you according to your iniquities, for it was I who was punished on a cross in your place. If you are waiting for more proof than this of My love for you, you will wait in vain. For there is no greater love than this: I died for you when you didn't love Me. Though you have feared Me for all the wrong reasons, as a father loves and thus pities his children, so have I loved and pitied you."

Immediately, I was gripped with a love so powerful that deep sobs engulfed me as the reality of what God had done—*for me*—flooded my soul. I knew I deserved to be "socked" with punishment and eternal separation from God, but He instead *sought* me and never gave up; I deserved to be "bopped" and left bound by my sin, but He *bought* me with a price unmatched by any other and set me free. And He went further: as far as sunrise is from sunset, so far has He removed my transgressions from me, and He remembers them no more.

I became like the woman in Luke 7 who couldn't stop weeping at Jesus' feet. Simon, the Pharisee who had invited Jesus to dinner, was aghast that Jesus would allow this sinful woman to be so demonstrative. But Jesus taught Simon the depth to which love will stoop and the transformation it brings. The sinful woman's demonstration of love was her recognition of how deeply God stooped to set her free. She humbly fell at His feet, realizing her unworthiness to stand face-to-face in His presence.

When my Teacher stooped down into the dust where sin had sprawled me, writing words of love and forgiveness, I, too, could only weep at His feet. Since then, the reality of His love for me has settled into my soul, transforming my life and erasing the warped concept I carried for years and replacing it with true knowledge of Him.

Some time ago, David and I traveled to Hawaii. One day as I sat on a high grassy slope watching the fierce waves crash against the shoreline, young parents walked up the hill pushing their baby daughter in a stroller. She was tiny—maybe six or eight months old. As they neared the crest of the hill, the baby began to scream with fear, for the crashing waves were loud and intense. The young father came to the front of her stroller and stooped down, bringing his face level with his daughter's. I heard him say, "Hey, there . . . ," then the noise of the waves drowned his voice. The father spoke gently, trying to quiet her, but she refused to be comforted. Soon, he loosened her straps and took her into his arms and turned to the waves as if to say, "There, I have you. Don't be afraid." As I took in that scene, a phrase of scripture came to mind, "If you, then, though you are evil, know how to give good gifts to your children, how much more will your Father in heaven give good gifts to those who ask him!" (Matt. 7:11).

Your deepest need is to know that you are loved by God. If you don't know it, you are likely to search for love in the wrong places to try to fill the hole in your heart. The search for love apart from God leads to sin, which leads to greater doubt of God's love, which brings more emptiness.

Whether you have outwardly committed sin or are inwardly contemplating it, you won't experience God's love unless you first confess it and receive His forgiveness. God stands ready to forgive. Perhaps your problem is not immorality. Maybe you are guilty of trying to polish your performance in an attempt to measure up so that God will love and accept you. This, too, can be confessed, for it is not God's way for you to try to achieve righteousness through good works. Only through trusting in His forgiveness do we come to realize that there is nothing we can do to deserve His love, nothing we can do to lessen its depth, nothing we can do to ever diminish it.

I lived in the Psalms for the first year following our divorce. It transformed my idea about God's love for me.

- Read one psalm each day, and make it personal by saying your own name and personal pronouns where appropriate. See the difference it makes.
- In your own Bible, turn to Ps. 103 and write out verses 1-13 using this technique.

There are times that, even though you have turned your back on your past and have submerged yourself in God's healing Word, the cries of your heart will not cease. I felt like this many, many times. When I did, I opened my journal and frantically wrote a love letter to me from God. As I wrote, I imagined that, just as the earthly father stooped down to soothe the cries of his baby daughter, my Heavenly Father stooped down to still my cries. In my journal, those letters from God started "Dear Lyndell."

- Write a letter to yourself from God.
- Let God tell you how much He loves you.
- Write God's words of forgiveness to you.
- Let God's words fill the void in your life.
- Write God's promises to you *personally* as they are found in His Word.

9

Who Is Carrying the Mountain?

*I*n the two years following my divorce—and especially following God's transforming work of forgiveness in my life—my eyes were opened to the enormous cost of adultery. Had I remained in my sin, or if I had remarried, I would not have seen the far-reaching stain it caused. Like Hester Prynne in *The Scarlet Letter*, everywhere I turned, a capital A left its mark. Do you think you fully understand the cost of adultery?

I firmly believe that none of us anticipates the high cost of adultery until we see its ugliness splashed across our lives. The painful scenes are unforgettable.

It is a lie that you can commit sexual immorality without hurting others.

Maybe you're getting away with adultery right now. But beware. It will swallow your life as you know it and severely damage the lives of those you love in tragic ways you cannot anticipate. It did mine. Even though God had forgiven me, the emotional cost of my adultery was shattering. I will never forget one night when, like a roaring beast, I wept bitterly before God as the consequence of my sin closed in on me: *Dear God! Help me! I am sinking, and I feel as if my fragile grip on sanity is slipping away. Please come to me, touch me—my fears, my shame, my losses overwhelm me tonight. I did not want this!*

I naively thought that I could commit adultery and no one would get hurt. I justified it by believing that as long as no one knows, no one gets hurt, and everything will be OK. It is amazing how dark and twisted my thinking became in the throes of my affair.

"Do not be deceived: God cannot be mocked" (Gal. 6:7). Our sins will be found out, and we will be left bearing the painful consequences. We reap what we sow.

Applying Truth

I will never forget the night my husband discovered my affair. I can never erase the memory of him on the floor, slumped against our bedroom wall with his head in his hands. For the first time in 25 years I saw him cry like a baby. For the first time in 25 years I held him and rocked him as he wept in my arms.

The first Christmas without David will be forever etched in my mind. Our four children and I were the only ones in our home on Christmas morning. Even though we were divorced by this time, David had planned to be present. However, he had left the night before, still unable to be in my presence without displaying his anger and hurt. So he had driven back to his home in Wisconsin. There was no joy in the faces of my children that morning. There was no eagerness, only deep sorrow that paled their faces and hushed their voices. It was as if someone they loved had died. Chad, the oldest, upheld tradition by taking his dad's place and began to read the story of Jesus' birth from the Gospel of Luke before we opened presents. His voice broke, but he finished the story as tears streamed down all our faces.

We lived in a small town, so it was inevitable that one day I would run into her. She had been my friend, but the look of betrayal and hurt that flashed from her eyes sent me running for cover. She was and still is the wife of the man I had an affair with. Her oldest children looked at me with distrust and wariness. Her mother-in-law, who was also a friend, snubbed me each time she saw me. I became a monster in their eyes, compounding my shame and guilt and isolating me further from people who were once my friends.

The ripple effect of our divorce reached far and wide. Having been active in the ministry and in our local church, there were many people who knew us and knew what we stood for. The year after our divorce, two prominent couples in our church divorced after long marriages of more than 20 years. My sister and her husband divorced—active members in their church. Friends were aghast, confused. Our home, our witness, and the message of the power of Christ to work miracles in our lives—a message we once lived and preached—was destroyed.

Facing my parents with my confession of adultery was one of the hardest things I have ever done. My parents celebrated their 54th anniversary this year. They have been faithful, loving, and generous Christian parents to me and my siblings. Their pride in me was something I cherished. My affair and subsequent divorce dropped a mountain of heartache and suffering on them.

And then there was me. What I did ultimately affected my soul. No matter how hard I tried, the two could not be separated. As a Christian, my entire body was a member of Christ's, for it was His shed blood that ransomed me from the penalty of death brought on by sin. Before creation, God's image was stamped upon my soul. In body and soul God had claimed me, and I was one with Him. Therefore, when I committed adultery, I joined the Body of Christ in an immoral act. (See 1 Cor. 6:13-16.) That is why, when we who have known and walked with Christ engage in immorality, we often feel as if our souls have been separated from the bodies—as if our psyches have been split down the middle. When we sin against another person, we create turmoil and separation in that relationship. When we as Christians sin against our own bodies, we sin against the body and spirit of Christ; therefore, we create the same environment of warfare—only within. Hence, Paul's warning, "Flee from sexual immorality. All other sins a man commits are outside his body, but he who sins sexually sins against his own body" (v. 18).

The Mountain

The destructive forces of immorality and divorce are incalculable. Who really stands to lose? The truth is, we all do. And this incredible loss, to you and to others, can never be imagined prior to an affair.

I recall a short story I read when I was in college that profoundly moved me. I don't remember the author or the title, but I have never forgotten the impact. The story was about a husband and father of teenage children who had fallen in love with another woman and had decided to leave his marriage and move in with her. The heart of the story was the father breaking the news to each of his children and their responses. As he broke the news to his oldest teenage son, he explained that he was leaving because he could no longer live with the burden of his marriage. He told his son that since he made the decision to leave, it was as if a huge mountain had been lifted from his shoulders. His son was still and silent for several moments, then with wisdom far greater than his dad possessed, he said, "But, Dad, you dumped the mountain on me."

Adultery and divorce rob our loved ones of the lives they have always known and have come to expect. We may have escaped the mountain, but it crushes them. Yes, everyone seems to eventually move on, but I believe that only eternity will reveal the hell that privately rages in the hearts of those we love.

In an article by Randy Alcorn, "Strategies to Keep from Falling," he wrote about a man who had been a leader in a Christian organization until he fell into immorality. He had the chance to ask this man, "What could have been done to prevent this?" The man paused for a moment, then with "haunting pain and precision" said, "If only I had really known, really thought through what it would cost me and my family and my Lord, I honestly believe I never would have done it."[1] This is your moment to think and to count the cost.

List the names of those who would experience immediate soul damage if you pursue a path of immorality.

Now list the specific, long-term damages that would occur relationally, socially, financially, and spiritually.

I realize there may be little impact in making these two lists. In 1 Tim. 4:1-2, we are told that our consciences become seared, and we can lose the ability to distinguish between right and wrong or to feel any concern about it. It is easy to convince ourselves that we will be the exception and that everyone will live happily ever after once the dust has settled.

It is interesting that a secular newspaper addressed this notion in an article reviewing a book written by Elizabeth Marquardt, *Between Two Worlds: The Inner Lives of Children of Divorce.* The book blows the lid off the world's lie that divorce can be happy with little trauma:

> A new book out this month presents compelling evidence that even a relatively amicable divorce cannot spare children from psychological

trauma that shapes their personalities into adulthood . . . for marriage gives kids one world . . . divorce forces them to inhabit two [creating a] divided self as they try to fit into two, separate parental realms. . . .

Children of divorce feel less protected by their parents, less emotionally secure, and less safe at home than do other children. . . . The "happy talk" about well-managed breakups lets adults dismiss and make light of children's real experiences.[2]

Could it be that a "seared conscience" allows once fiercely protective parents to lightly dismiss the psychological trauma that is dumped upon their children because of immorality and divorce that is often inevitable? Don't let the world and the media and Hollywood convince you that leaving your marriage is insignificant to the lives of your children. Don't be fooled by the lie that your children will be better off or that adult children recover more quickly.

I never fully understood the depth of sorrow our oldest son felt as a result of our divorce until I witnessed the incredible joy on his face the day David and I remarried. He sobbed behind us throughout the ceremony. He was 28.

Regardless of what we may or may not *feel,* this is the truth from God's Word, "It is God's will that you should be sanctified: that you should avoid sexual immorality. . . . For God did not call us to be impure, but to live a holy life" (1 Thess. 4:3, 7).

You don't reject your church or your spouse, you reject God if you persist in immorality. Ultimately, it is not about you and your spouse or you and another person; it is about you and God. Who will be in charge? Who will have the final say? Whose truth will you embrace? The world's? Your own, that springs from a seared conscience?

Adultery sears our consciences, sucks energy from our spirits, and severely damages our souls. When I was facedown in the dust of my sin and shame, only then did I realize how far I had fallen. God had a lot of cleaning up to do. How I longed for a clean conscience and a new heart within! If you desire the same, then it is imperative that you get into the Word of God. Flesh that is seared and the resulting scar have no feeling. It is the same with a seared conscience. It takes a long time for demonic strongholds to weaken their grip and eventually disappear so that you can think and feel rightly again. But God does it, and here is what He says:

> I will sprinkle clean water on you, and you will be clean; I will cleanse you from all your impurities and from all your idols. I will give you a new heart and put a new spirit in you; I will remove from you your heart of stone and give you a heart of flesh. And I will put my Spirit in you

and move you to follow my decrees and be care-
ful to keep my laws *(Ezek. 36:25-27)*.

The Trampling of a Great Love

When I began to feel again; to *feel* the abomination of what I had done, I realized that, though my
sin cost me dearly, it paled in comparison to what it
cost Christ to forgive. And I had crucified Him all over
again. Yet I remain deeply humbled by how He came
to me that night.

My "roaring beast" scene had taken place in my
car, in the dark, on a deserted hill near where I lived. I
had rolled up the windows and screamed out my despair. Finally, spent of all emotion, a dead calm settled
over me. I rolled down the window and looked across
the starlit fields. A bright moon was casting a glow all
around me. Immediately, I sensed God was there. Not
overwhelmingly so—just quietly there with these comforting words, "Fear not: for, behold, I bring you good
tidings of great joy . . . For unto you is born this day . . .
a Saviour . . . ye shall find the babe wrapped in swad-
dling clothes, lying in a manger" (Luke 2:10-12, KJV).

He came quietly into my blackest night, into the
lowly manger that was my life. He came, and He
wrapped His love around me, telling me to "fear not"
for a Savior had come and He was in my midst. And
though I couldn't imagine how, He alone would restore joy to my broken life.

This is the love we trample on when we throw caution to the wind and pursue a path of immorality. But there will come a day when His love will no longer woo us but judge us. You may still think you can get away with it—that no one knows—no one is hurt. But, friend, may you never forget: there is One who sees, One who is deeply grieved, One who *is* counting the cost.

10

The False God Eros

Adultery happens because it is a pleasurable pursuit. Even considering the energy it takes to maintain an adulterous relationship, the pleasure often outweighs the sacrifice. Hebrews does not refer to sin as a passing *pain* but rather a passing *pleasure* (11:25). The romance, love, and passion that have disappeared in marriage are rediscovered in a new relationship. Convinced these new feelings won't fade—like the old ones did—we trade the old problems for new ones. Believe me: the pleasure found in adultery will eventually pass, and the new place in which you find yourself will strongly resemble the place you left. This new god you bow to is not trustworthy. Yet many are banking a brand-new future on it and are sacrificing an entire history to it.

This was made very clear to me when David and I attended several weekend retreats for couples whose marriages were on the brink of divorce. David and I were already divorced, and these weekends were a strong link in our journey toward reconciliation.

It was interesting that many of these couples were attending to try to save their second marriages. As they shared their stories, it wasn't hard to read between the lines: Both had left their former mates for this new relationship. And now it was falling apart.

Peggy Vaughn, an author and expert on second marriages, says, "The chances of having a successful marriage that began from an affair is about like winning the lottery—possible for a rare few, but not something any sensible person would bet on."[1]

Anne Kass, a district judge in New Mexico, has witnessed the demise of many second marriages—especially those involving stepchildren. Based on her experience, they fail for a number of reasons: Ongoing financial problems resulting from the first divorce, complications from the blended family, and keeping the peace in all the new relationships. In her courtroom she has heard people say, "If I had tried half as hard to make my first marriage work as I have tried to make this one work, I could have survived." One man, divorcing for the second time, recently said of his first divorce: "I hurt my kids. I lost my home, and the problems my first wife and I had weren't much different from the problems my second wife and I have." Kass concludes her article by saying, "If only there were some way to get people to realize all this without their having to experience it firsthand."[2]

This truth about second marriages is even captured in secular poetry, such as the following by Daisy Goodwin:

> *In rooms whose lights*
> *On winter evenings*
> *Make peepshows of our lives—*
> *Behind each window*
> *A stage so cluttered up*
> *With props and furniture*
> *It's not surprising*
> *We make a mess of what began*
> *So simply with I love you.*
> *Look at us: some*
> *Slumped in chairs*
> *And hardly ever speaking*
> *And others mouthing*
> *The same tired lines to ears*
> *That long ago stopped listening.*
> *Once we must have dreamed*
> *Of something better.*
> *But even those who swapped*
> *One partner for another*
> *Have ended up*
> *Just like the rest of us.*[3]

Eros Unplugged

Recently I went deep-sea fishing, or I should say others went fishing while I and four other shipmates puked into little white bags. As I lay there, wishing I could die, I noticed that the healthy ones were having a grand time hauling one fish after another onto the boat. In spite of my miserable condition, I felt sorry for the fish as they were tossed into an orange basket—flopping and jerking—then, except for their rapid breathing, they became suddenly still, as if they knew of the inevitable death that was soon to come. Obviously, on many levels I lack the stomach to fish! Regardless of how you feel about fishing, it highlights at least one truth: The fish ends up dead in an orange basket because it did not know that the enticing lure it went for was but a passing pleasure that would lead to its death.

The hook of romantic love that at one time led us to the altar compelled us to pledge undying love and commitment to the one next to us. The thought of this love costing us something never entered our romantic heads, for this love brought such pleasure to self that we didn't mind sacrificing for the other. How does a love that powerful die? How do we get from there to falling out of love with our spouse and into love with someone else?—the number one reason for having an affair and divorcing.

I think it's because we fail to realize that, just as the biting of the hook ultimately led the fish to death, the hook of eros love that brought us to marriage must ultimately lead to a death of sorts—the death of the self-centered, all-about-me self—if the marriage is to thrive and survive.

When we are in the grip of eros love, notice how central *I* and *me* are to the thinking. "*I* have never been so happy." "He makes *me* feel alive." "His love completes *me*." We will ride the powerful wave of eros love as long as it delivers those wonderful strokes to the self, but when the strokes stop, so does our willingness to sacrifice.

What we see today in marriages in Hollywood and even in our churches is what happens when the strokes stop. Marriages are crashing like waves. We fall out of love and out of our marriages because we fail to realize there is another love to fall into: agape love—God's kind of love. Eros is kindergarten love when compared to agape love. Eros love gets us to the altar; agape love places us *on* the altar of loving sacrifice. Agape love asks us to grow up and empty ourselves of our own self-centered love in order to receive God's unselfish, other-centered love that will carry us into genuine and enduring love. In every relationship, we must at some point plug into God's agape love if we are to experience the love life that God intended for us.

The Myth of Warmer Lips

Because we fail to strive for agape love, we keep putting our trust in the god of eros, hoping that this time it will give us "happily ever after." But it leads to deaths of a different kind—deaths of marriages, families, and history. We become disillusioned in marriage where love has died, and because we do not realize that the death of "all about me" is what is needed, we swim away from what agape love demands of us. Instead of paying the price, we force everyone around us to pay the price. As eros love loses its motivating power, and we realize there is a cost involved, we flop about in our emotions, we struggle, we resist, we put up walls, demand our rights, demand our way, refuse to be the first to give, until things become hopeless and we begin to look for another hook in another pond. Lured away by powerful feelings, we bow to the god of eros and bring death to a promise we made and end up doing things we once thought we were incapable of doing.

But warmer lips become cold also—just like in the former relationship. The dollars have to be stretched, there is still laundry, there is still a job to be tended to, there is still a house to clean, there are still children's school and sport schedules to juggle. Only now all that is doubled; plus there will likely be stepchildren and stepparenting added to the mix.

The Rest of the Story

It would be a mistake to imply that our self-centeredness and our idolization of eros love are the only driving powers behind our search for *happily ever after.* Based upon my own experience, I believe there is another force even more powerful taking place. The fact that reality was waiting to burst my bubble was not enough to deter me. Knowing that my actions were sinful and selfish did not steer me away from the broad path that led to destruction. Being sinfully self-centered may explain why I did what I did, but it is not the whole answer. Rather, it's the power of the *wound* behind the wound of adultery that often drives us.

Dr. Willard Harley writes in *His Needs, Her Needs:*

> Early in my career as a counselor I often felt dismayed to see people with strong religious and moral commitments becoming involved in extramarital affairs. I am a church member myself, with strong convictions about the Christian faith. How could people who claim to have the same commitment go astray? Did their faith lack power? The more I dealt with Christian clients and other people with deep moral convictions, the more I understood the power of our basic emotional needs.[4]

In an adulterous relationship, that which exerts the most power in a woman's life is not the relationship itself; rather, it is a life and marriage wounded by the absence of love that makes her vulnerable to such a relationship to fulfill this powerful need.

Remember—the fish bites because it's *hungry.* It seems that women more than men will grab that hook because their souls are hungry for love and, instinctively, they know they cannot live without it. We seek to fill the hole in our hearts with the love and comfort a new relationship promises: someone who listens to me, who understands me, who appreciates me. But it all comes down to the need to love and be loved. Beneath the surface, our behavior is a driving fear that says, *I am unloved, unworthy, and powerless to do anything about it.* The god of adultery promises us power and convinces us that the comfort we need, the personal worth, happiness, and love we seek, is wrapped up in another person.

I was no exception. All my life I had a deep hunger to be loved but did not know it. I had wonderful, loving parents, but I grew up convinced that I was in need of no one. I was stubborn, independent, and often aloof in my marriage. Unknowingly, I built walls to keep love out. It wasn't until I became intimately involved in a relationship that started as a friendship that I recognized my deep need to be loved. I was both surprised and stunned by love and my hunger for it. It was as if a scab had been removed from my heart, revealing overwhelming needs and longings that had never been allowed to surface. When an adulterous relationship awakens this need, you believe you cannot live without the one who has brought it to life. The relationship becomes as necessary to your survival as the air you breathe and the food you eat. That's why emotional affairs are like addictions and so difficult to break.

It is a lie that the hunger that drives
you to adultery will be satisfied
by the new relationship.

Part of the reason David and I divorced is because after the affair ended my husband did not understand my grief. At the time, I didn't understand it either. For months I was like a zombie, going through the motions of life. In this shattered state, I signed divorce papers, became physically sick, wasted away to skin and bones; I was lifeless, spiritless, joyless, hopeless. I remember feeling amazed that one's body could be in so much pain and still be alive.

My soul knew what it hungered for: not eros love but God's eternal, healing love. How my soul must have cringed as I reached for a temporary fix that could only treat the symptoms but never touch the root of my hunger. Sadly, when we are ignorant of what the soul truly hungers for, it leads to desperate and tragic decisions.

The Claiming Fires of Eros

Though two undeniable realities may exist in our lives—a soul bereft of love and a spousal love that has died—trusting in the limited parameters of eros love is a tragic mistake. We often fail to anticipate missing what we sacrifice to the god of eros until it is too late.

In the process of writing this chapter, I received a call from a friend who asked me to pray for a woman in her church. The woman has been a Christian wife, mother, and a leader in her church and has been married almost 30 years to a wonderful Christian man. A month ago, she left her husband. In conversation with my friend, this woman admitted there is someone else, a secret she has kept from everyone. Because of this attraction, she is unwilling to consider any of the spiritual guidance my friend is attempting to give her. Her response is, "I just don't want to go there." My friend asked me, "How do you get someone who *wants* to stay blind to see the truth?" Such is the power of eros love.

It is not within my power or my friend's power to get this woman to turn from eros love to a greater love. She has arrived at a dangerous place. She now loves darkness more than light because she knows her deeds are evil, and she does not want them to be exposed to the truth. (See John 3:19-20.) We can only faithfully and fervently pray as we helplessly watch her grope, as the blind man gropes in darkness. As we are warned in Deut. 28:29, she shall not prosper in her ways, she will be oppressed, and she will be robbed continually, with none to save her. Blinded by the grip of eros love, I guarantee that she does not anticipate missing the life that Satan will rob her of. Like others have tragically discovered, she will become aware too late.

Two days before this phone call, I ran into a woman I had met in a divorce care group. After more than 30 years of marriage, her husband had left her for a much younger woman. A long and agonizing divorce has now been finalized. Although she is doing remarkably well since I last saw her, she is still learning to cope with being single after so many years of marriage. I asked her how her former husband was faring; he never married the *other woman* but was living with her. This was her reply, "Two nights ago, he called me to apologize for everything he has done. He said if he had it to do over again, he never would have left me. He now realizes he made a mistake, and he asked if he could come home and try to work things out." She told him no; that door is closed forever. She has moved on without him. She has no desire to reconcile. Furthermore, his adult children want nothing to do with him. Being sorry too late has cost this man his home and entire family.

Another incident similar to this occurred about four years ago in another family we know well. A young wife and mother left her family for another man. Three years later, she realized her mistake and wanted to come home to the husband and daughter she abandoned. But by then, the husband was deeply involved with someone else. He has since married, and he and his new wife have a child together. His former wife, now alone, is devastated. She still struggles to get past this great loss and move on with her life.

I think of another man who left his first wife for another woman. Ten years later, his second wife left him for another man. Realizing his mistake, he turned to his former wife, desiring to reconcile. Though still single, she has moved so far beyond her prior life with him that she wants nothing to do with him. In his mid 60s, he now finds himself completely alone in life—and filled with regrets.

Each of us could tell similar stories that remind us of a truer reality than the happily-ever-after one anticipated with a new partner. These stories of how willing we are to sacrifice our families to the god of eros in pursuit of love and happiness reminds me of how similar our actions are to the Israelites of Ezekiel's day. God likens Israel to an unfaithful wife because of her practice of idolatry and her alliances with foreign countries, which led Israel to engage in unthinkable behavior. In Ezek. 16:20-21, we hear God's greatest condemnation: "Moreover, you took your sons and daughters whom you had borne to Me and sacrificed them to idols to be devoured. . . . You slaughtered My children and offered them up to idols by causing them to pass through the fire" (NASB). Though we protest that we are much more civilized today and would never engage in such activity, we are doing much the same thing when we bow to the god of eros and align ourselves with someone other than our spouse. The same devourer that has us in the grip of passing pleasures is the same devourer to whom we offer up our families—causing them to pass through the fire, bringing death to a family and its history.

I never realized how precious our family history was until David and I stopped creating it. I have since come to realize that when couples marry they begin a history together—a precious legacy. When children are born into this unique stream of history, it is cemented and becomes even more sacred and significant. When a spouse leaves, even if the miracle of reconciliation occurs, this history is disrupted; it will not move forward in the same way ever again. What is also lost is how that history shaped and defined us as a wife, a mother, and as a human being. We are intimately and intricately connected with it. You may be unable to imagine missing the role that once defined you, but I guarantee, you will. We can never go back and resume our former roles and step into the pages of history that surround our families again. The history we had a key role in beginning will now end in a place different from where it began. This history that we helped start will now move in different directions, creating new streams. Once major players in the mainstream, we now share that role with other major players in new and unfamiliar streams, sweeping our children away in directions over which we have no control. Often, it is not until many years later that we realize that we sacrificed it all to an outrageous lie—to the god of eros whose fire claimed everything dear and sacred in our lives.

Does this sound overly dramatic? I hope so. In our lives today we tend to be overly dramatic about things that do not matter one iota. But if we become ensnared in an adulterous relationship, we will find ourselves knee-deep in excessive drama. It is about time we are excessively dramatic—militant even—about saving our families; about going to any length, any measure to keep them out of the grip of the devourer.

In Mal. 2:14-16 the Lord warns:

> Because the LORD is acting as the witness between you and the wife of your youth, because you have broken faith with her, though she is your partner, the wife of your marriage covenant.

Has not the LORD made them one? In flesh and spirit they are his. And why one? Because he was seeking godly offspring. So guard yourself in your spirit, and do not break faith with the wife of your youth. "I hate divorce," says the LORD God of Israel, "and I hate a man's covering himself with violence as well as with his garment," says the LORD Almighty. So guard yourself in your spirit, and do not break faith.

In this chapter, God tells the Israelites that He will no longer accept their offerings, and their refusal to face up to the seriousness of divorce is one of the reasons He gave. The garment spoken of is a symbol of protection for the spouse and family. When we cover this garment with wrongdoing, such as infidelity or divorce, we are removing the garment of protection from our spouse and family, exposing them to the destructive flames of bitterness, anger, unnecessary heartache, and enormous loss.

A Second Chance

God's agape love exists so that we may be spared from such tragic and irreversible decisions. Fortunately, God gave me a second chance to make history with my family. Though undeserving, I am so grateful that God granted me the opportunity to restore the garment of faithfulness, love, and commitment. The second chance has opened my eyes to things I foolishly took for granted, important things I didn't anticipate missing; moments that are now precious in my sight:

- Sitting with my family at the Thanksgiving table
- Traveling to Pennsylvania together to spend Christmas with our dear parents
- Sitting side-by-side at our daughter's wedding
- The surprise party David threw on my 50th birthday
- David and I reveling together in the joy of our first grandchild
- Participating in the dedication ceremony of our second grandson
- The anticipation we share as we look forward to the birth of more grandchildren
- Sitting on the beach together at the Outer Banks with our children and grandchildren surrounding us
- David and I kneeling with our daughter as she gave her life to Christ
- David's comfort and support when my grandmother passed away
- Sitting in church together
- Taking Communion together
- Holding hands and praying together for our children, grandchildren, family, and friends

This agape love that is poured out in my heart for my husband cannot fail or die. It is a powerful love that keeps transforming me from a taker to a giver who seeks only to improve the condition of another. It is joy found on the other side of self-centeredness that makes mere happiness look like a beggar's crumb. It is a deep fulfillment that comes from being a person of integrity—a person who knows what it means to speak words of faithfulness and commitment and to keep those words regardless of the cost. It is healing that has brought deep contentment to a love-starved soul. And in the process, I have found the love of my life that God intended me to find all along.

Applying Truth

In *Living with Unfulfilled Desires,* Walter Trobisch says, "The task we have to face is the same, whether we are married or single: to live a fulfilled life in spite of many unfulfilled desires."[5] What is common today, even among Christians, is that most people are just not willing to live with it. They have concluded that living with self-denial is too high a price to pay, especially when they see others opting for the easy way out through extramarital affairs. I know the argument. I've heard it, and I've wailed it. "You just don't understand!" But turning to adultery to fill the hole in our hearts shows that we are the ones who don't understand. Make no mistake; it requires a massive trade-off.

- It requires that you trade your faithfulness for unfaithfulness.
- It requires that you trade the truth for falsehood.
- It requires that you trade your promises for promiscuity.
- It requires that you trade your integrity for deceitfulness.
- It requires you to trade your faith for apostasy.
- It requires you to trade the happiness of others for your own happiness.
- It requires you to trade the wisdom of God for the lies of Satan.
- It requires you to trade heaven for hell.

Steep price? Yes, it is indeed a steep price to pay to satisfy the hunger within.

We need to be reminded that a steep price has already been paid by another who longs to become the only lover of our souls. God's love is the only love that satisfies our deepest hunger. We don't have to pay the price to get the love we need; no one else need pay the price to give us what we need. When the unmet desires are screaming and it appears hopeless, remember that He died for our hour of lovelessness. I have come to know this as a blessed reality. It was during my period of healing and restoration that my soul discovered what it had longed for all along.

Several months into my affair, I broke it off.

However, my emotions were deeply ensnared by then, and I grieved for what I had lost. One day, God spoke clearly to me, "You have lost nothing; you have been spared everything." How I wish I had heeded those words, but I did not. After my divorce, I recalled that moment when my Heavenly Father tried to love me by steering my life away from the day when I lost *everything* to nothing.

If we could only realize that God's commands are for our protection and peace, for rest and comfort, for blessings and not cursings, for life and not death, for genuine love and true fulfillment. He commands obedience, for He also loves our spouses and our children—the history He has blessed us with. He loves the one we are tempted to be unfaithful with and his or her family. He loves those watching who would be shocked and devastated by our sin. He wants to spare us all from the needless pain and ruin our sin will cause. How ironic that the love we find in adultery destroys love in every other area of our lives. God wants to spare us from trampling on the love He has given to us.

But I have come to learn that God's love is also for the one whose love has died. The journey to David and me loving one another again was incredibly hard and painful. When I came back to David to reconcile, I had no love, no feelings for him. Though I clearly deserved the things he said and did after the discovery of my affair, the words had stripped away any last shred of love and respect I had for him. A journal entry I made two months after I moved to St. Louis to reconcile with David reveals the impossible challenge we faced to love one another again. To see us today is to see the miracle of agape love.

We fought last night. The anger and same old accusations from David surfaced again—How could you have done what you did? I fired back— How could you have treated me like you did? On and on we vented. Finally, he stormed out of the house and I began to pack my stuff. I was leaving—heading back to PA. As I packed, I wept. I felt a voice inside, urging me to not do this. I knew it was the Spirit's voice. I sank down on the floor, weeping. So tired! Weary of the struggle. I wanted to run—to escape. But at the same time the voice was saying: "Hold fast to the Word. Trust me. Humble yourself under my mighty hand. Cast all your cares upon me." All the verses I had been memorizing came raining down upon my soul. I kept trying to bat them away. I didn't want to listen. I had enough. But soon, I began to melt: "Oh Lord! Help me, help us! Help my heart be tender. Keep me willing. Make me willing to seek only your way, because right now I am not willing!" Soon I was unpacking, putting clothes away only because I was convinced that God was close

*by, that His words were in my mouth, in my heart,
and His hand was guiding me, even though outwardly I was a mess—torn, confused, despairing.
Just as calm began to settle over me, David came
home, and once again angry words, accusations
were flying. Then stonewall silence from him. Fervently, I began to pack again, this time crying, "I
am leaving for a few days. I need to get a way
from here to think. I can't continue to go on like
this." I heard the Spirit whisper again: "Today if
you hear His voice do not harden your hearts."
Yes, I could feel my heart beginning to harden.
But I persisted, stubbornly packing. I moved into
the guest room and bedded down for the night.
Sullen, withdrawn, and hurting. But I didn't feel
good about it. All the while I felt the Holy Spirit's
gentle nudging—like a shepherd who nudges a
willful and headstrong lamb back into the fold—
my shepherd was nudging me. As I fell asleep, I
prayed, "Oh Lord, help me. Help us."*

*The next day, I didn't leave. Instead, we
talked in great length. I cried as I shared my feelings or lack of feelings toward him. He wants
more than I can give—I want him to give me time
and not pressure me into saying what I can't say—
into doing what I can't do. The fact that I am
here, simply here, is all I can give. I can't offer
more. We committed again to each other and to*

the process, though my commitment was weak and shaky, for in my heart I did not want to stay. Yet at the same time I realized deep down that this is what I really want! I want to love this man. I want to grow old with him. Create a home together with joy, warmth, and tenderness. I can't imagine David and me going our separate ways and building two separate lives apart. I recalled the love I once had for him. But now I say that this love has died, that I am no longer "in love." In many ways we are just like all the famous, beautiful couples we see in the media. Couples who once declared undying love are all-too-soon declaring divorce because "love has died" and they have found a new love and are moving out and moving on. We are Christians, yet we are living like the ungodly, as if another kind of love never existed at all! But there is another kind of love and it walked through the door later that night. David walked in with a huge and carefully wrapped gift, and I unfolded the most beautiful dozen red roses I had ever seen. I wept. Here was a man I had said earlier I was not "in love" with—that the past two years had erased all feelings and respect. And in walks agape love, carefully wrapped with tenderness and love.

Though there were many challenging scenes to come, that night was a turning point. I had prayed that God would break down all the barriers that kept me from receiving His love and giving it to David. In light of agape love in action, I saw that the real barriers were my ingratitude and self-centeredness. Deeply convicted, I could only pray, "Forgive me, Lord. Change *me!*" I realized that only God's agape love could transform me by pouring in the very character of Christ:

- A positive attitude toward David rather than a negative one
- A decision to give of myself, regardless what I felt
- A commitment that said, "I am committed to this marriage and will not leave no matter how painful the process of reconciliation becomes"
- Faithfulness that forsook all others and clung only to David
- Faith in God's Word as the only measure of what real love feels like and looks like

God has taught me that real love is not at all about feelings. Rather, it is about forsaking my *all-about-me* needs in order to bring joy to another. When I did, the most incredible thing occurred: the feelings found me. Placing my feelings last and the feelings of my husband first eventually brought the feelings of a deep and genuine love.

Have you faced your need for love? Many of us stumble along in life, realizing that we thirst, but we never identify the thirst. To be blindsided by our thirst is to never be conscious of the choices we make to quench it. When my affair met unfulfilled needs, I believed it was another person who discovered and awakened these needs, but they were really always there. By not facing them and feeling their absence, I never gave my husband or God a chance to fulfill them. What the soul ultimately wants is God's love! Once we recognize the need and acknowledge God as the only source to meet it, He begins to fill us. As we begin to see God's loving hand covering our lives, we move even closer to its warmth. We sense we are no longer alone. As He fills us with His love, we hunger and thirst for more of it. We come to realize that it is unparalleled to anything we have ever experienced. Perhaps you have built walls to keep love out—from your spouse and from God. Once you let Him in, you will exclaim as I did, "So this is what wholeness looks like. This is freedom!"

- In what ways have you sought in vain for love?
- Meditate on the following verses and then open the doors to your heart, mind, and soul to receive the love you have read about. Once you have opened up to His love, write out what you feel the Spirit is saying to you through these verses: 2 Chron. 5:13; Neh. 9:17; Ps. 13:5; 18:1; 25:7; 31:21; 103:4; 119:76; Isa. 38:17; 63:9; Jer. 31:3; 32:18; Lam. 3:22; Hos.

2:23; 6:4; 11:4; John 15:13; Rom. 5:5-8; Eph. 3:18; Philem. 1:7; 1 John 3:1; 4:16; 4:18.

Only when we truly know God's love for us personally can we genuinely offer the same love to others. When we no longer feel love for our spouse, we need God's love to fall into. There is no downside to agape love—no matter the outcome. If the outcome is like mine—with love for my husband reborn and my relationship restored—then agape love has not failed. But if you steadfastly love with agape love and your marriage still fails because the other is resistant, then agape love still has not failed. Though you may grieve, where hate, bitterness, and anger could have reigned, forgiveness and mercy reign instead. Where a poisoned spirit could have ruled your entire life, a spirit of sweetness possesses you instead.

If your love has died, have you confessed this to God and to yourself? That's the first step. Then surrender to loving your spouse with God's agape love. Seek it with all your heart. Scrutinize your actions so that you can see the areas in which *you* need to change. Remember that agape love is other-centered and is done entirely apart from feelings. Do you think Christ *felt* like going to the Cross? If you seek feelings, they will elude you. Feelings are transient. If I only exercised when I felt like it, believe me, I would never exercise.

- If agape love ruled your life from here on out,

what changes do you think it would bring about in you?

- In your husband?
- In your relationship?
- Are you willing to surrender your feelings to Jesus and let Him create the feelings in you He wants according to His way?
- If so, write out your surrender as a prayer.

11

The Tragedy of What Might Have Been

My husband recently befriended a man whose wife of 25 years had left him for another man. This couple had been leaders in their church and had taught Bible studies in their home for many years. One day, the man came home and found a three-page letter on the kitchen table that turned his life and the lives of his two teenage children upside down. The letter from his wife said that she had found her soul mate. It detailed how sorry she was that she could no longer stay in a loveless marriage. But here was the jaw dropper: She went on to say that her decision was God's will. It was God's will that she had met this man, that God had brought this love into her life. Her reasoning was that God desires our happiness. Weeks have passed without a word from this once attentive wife and mother. Such unspeakable behavior has left us all stunned.

Unfortunately, we have been stunned before. Many years ago, in our third pastorate, two respected, faithful leaders in our church began an adulterous relationship. They were church board members, Sunday School teachers, and choir members. Yet they both walked away from long marriages and the church to begin a life together. In an effort to turn them away from their intended course, my husband delivered one last wake-up call to them privately in his office, but there was no dissuading them, for they were convinced that God was on their side. As they sat in David's office holding hands, they both explained that they had gotten down on their knees and prayed about this. Their prayers led them to the conclusion that this was God's will, for God desired their happiness, and they had found happiness in one another. They moved in together and married a year later. To my knowledge, neither has been in church again. The last information I received regarding this couple was that there was trouble in paradise.

There is a part of me that understands all too well the twisted line of thinking espoused by the betrayers. It is another case of seared consciences. Loved ones we once fiercely protected are now sacrificed in the pursuit of our own happiness. However, I can't understand how a Christian's thinking can become so warped that sin suddenly becomes God's will. I was living in denial about the perversity of my actions, but

I believe that the fact that I always knew adultery was sin gave God room to eventually perform a broken and contrite spirit within me.

The Big Picture

One day, God revealed to me in Scripture just how ludicrous such excuses are and what is tragically at stake. By applying this sordid line of thinking to Joseph's encounter with Potiphar's wife, we might not only see its absurdity but also recognize that what is at stake is bigger than we can ever imagine. It is the tragedy of what might have been.

Joseph was a handsome man—in form and appearance according to Scripture. Obviously, Potiphar's wife was smitten—so much so that "day by day" she tempted Joseph to "lie with her." And day after day, Joseph spurned her. Miffed, she sets Joseph up and falsely accuses him of the deed she had been begging for. Potiphar casts Joseph into prison where he is basically forgotten for two years. You can read the entire story of Joseph in Gen. 37—45.

But let's imagine another scenario that might have occurred had Joseph responded differently. Imagine one day Potiphar arriving home and finding a three-page letter on the kitchen table:

Dear Potiphar:

I first want to say what a wonderful Master you have been. Thank you for taking me under your wing, for trust-

*ing me with your household affairs and for believing in
me. I partially owe you for helping me become the man I
am today. However, it is time for me to be truthful with
you. Something has occurred that I did not foresee in a
dream, nor did I have the power to stop it. Your wife and I
have fallen in love with each other, and we have left to
build a brand-new life together. Now I see why God allowed me to suffer—why He allowed my brothers to kid-
nap me and throw me into a deep pit—why I was sold into
slavery and why God placed me in charge of your household. It was in order to meet your wife! It was God's will
that we found one another. Because God is in this, He will
take care of you and the trauma that occurs because of our
decision. Please don't send your chariots after us, for remember, God is on our side.*

Sincerely, Joseph

Laughable and, of course, ludicrous, but no more
ludicrous than the twisted "faith" we concoct and feed
to ourselves and our mates when we want something
that is in direct conflict with God's known will. Imagine
if Joseph had taken such a path far removed from God's
purpose. What follows would never have occurred.

Many years had passed and a great famine gripped
the land. Thousands were dying of starvation. Joseph's
father sends the remaining brothers to Egypt to pur-
chase grain so that "we may live and not die." Arriving
in Egypt, they are greeted by Joseph who had been elevated to the highest level of command under Pharaoh

due to his wisdom and faithfulness. Though his brothers do not recognize him, Joseph recognizes his brothers. After several visits with his brothers to negotiate for grain, Joseph one day could no longer control his emotions. He shouts to everyone but his brothers:

"Have everyone go out from me." So there was no man with him when Joseph made himself known to his brothers. He wept so loudly that the Egyptians heard it, and the household of Pharaoh heard it. Then Joseph said to his brothers, "I am Joseph! Is my father still alive?" But his brothers could not answer him, for they were dismayed at his presence. Then Joseph said to his brothers, "Please come closer to me." And they came closer. And he said, "I am your brother Joseph, whom you sold into Egypt. Now do not be grieved or angry with yourselves, because you sold me here, for God sent me before you to preserve life. For the famine has been in the land these two years, and there are still five years in which there will be neither plowing nor harvesting. God sent me before you to preserve for you a remnant in the earth, and to keep you alive by a great deliverance. Now, therefore, it was not you who sent me here, but God; and He has made me a father to Pharaoh and lord of all his household and ruler over all the land of Egypt" (Gen. 45:1-8, NASB).

This beautiful account of deliverance, forgiveness, and reconciliation would never have occurred had Joseph succumbed to the advances of Potiphar's wife. Faith in a big God kept Joseph focused on God's big picture. But it was not easy. Because he refused to succumb to the daily temptation to be unfaithful, Joseph endured suffering. He endured false accusations. He endured imprisonment—only to eventually be exalted to the highest position of authoritative power under Pharaoh. From this exalted place, Joseph was in a position to "preserve life" for his loved ones "by a great deliverance" in the midst of famine that gripped the earth. A major link in the deliverance of the lives of Joseph's family would have been missing had Joseph pursued his own will, happiness, and desires. Joseph's family would have reaped the tragedy of what might have been.

> *It is a lie that your adultery is God's will because He wants you to be happy.*

Similarly, when we depart from our marriages in order to pursue our happiness, convinced that it is not only wrapped up in someone new but also that it is God's will, something of great magnitude is robbed from the lives of our loved ones and it is this: *intercessory prayer and the righteous presence of a godly parent is absent from the lives of our children and our family.* It is impossible to walk a path in defiance to God's known will and still intercede for those we love. When famine comes into their lives, who will stand in the gap in order to preserve spiritual and eternal life for them? Who can better pray for your children than you? Who better cares for their eternal destiny than you? Who will intercede daily for them so that they may be delivered from sin and included in the remnant that one day Jesus will claim for all eternity?

We cannot allow ourselves to be deluded. When we take such an immoral path and flaunt it in the face of God, God will turn His face away from our prayers (see Isa. 59:2, NASB). But more importantly, the spirit of prayer is blunted within us, making us insensitive to the spiritual plights of our children. The blind cannot lead the blind. As Jesus warned, both will fall into the pit (see Matt. 15:14).

Applying Truth

Adultery breeds famine and division. I am speaking as one who has clearly been there, done that. When I was in the midst of an affair, I turned from being faithfully absorbed in the physical, emotional, and spiritual welfare of my children to being completely self-absorbed. My self-absorption left no room or energy for others. I retreated from contact with close Christian friends; I stopped mailing birthday cards; I stopped mailing the annual Christmas letter that had always chronicled God's blessings in our lives. I stopped praying.

My unrighteous life gave me no leg to stand on when my adult children were flailing morally. Our daughter got pregnant out of wedlock during this time. Our oldest son and his wife divorced. Our other son moved away to Las Vegas to work in a nightclub and is still there. Our youngest daughter struggled in her relationships, afraid of commitment: "If divorce can happen to you and Dad, what chance do we have?" Everything good in our lives was unraveling, and through it all, I coasted. I grew coldhearted and calloused. I brushed everything aside that stood in my way or demanded even the tiniest bit of sacrifice on my part. Nothing touched me or moved me except my hunger for a relationship that was, in reality, preying upon precious lives and creating famine all around me.

I realize that the events in my children's lives could have occurred even had I remained faithful, but what haunts me is that I will never know. Had I been faithfully praying, standing in the gap, would they be reaping the consequences they are today? Though I do not know, I do know this: something will always die as the result of an adulterous relationship. The story of King David and Bathsheba taught us this. Our tragedy most likely will not be the death of one of our children, as it was for David, but I guarantee that your love for God and His people will die. Your thirst for righteousness, your burden for the lost, your desire for prayer, and the ability to care all die as we pursue a willful path that is in direct opposition to God's will. Furthermore, I believe that the death of King David's firstborn stands as a warning symbolizing the spiritual and relational deaths that take place in a home ripped apart due to infidelity and divorce. King David's family knew nothing but strife and war till the day he died. An irreparable relationship existed between he and his son Absalom—that still was unresolved at Absalom's tragic death, leading David to voice one of the most soul-wrenching cries in all of Scripture: "O my son Absalom, my son, my son Absalom! Would I had died instead of you, O Absalom, my son, my son!" (2 Sam. 18:33, NASB).

Today, it is no different. I served as co-leader for the divorce care group in our church. Most of the attendees were there because of their spouse's adultery. As each new group gathered at the beginning of our 13-week session, the pain was so real you could slice it with a knife. Never have I encountered so much grief, anger, bitterness, and loss. Parents and children who once enjoyed a peaceful home environment were suddenly immersed in an all-out war and struggling to survive. Children as young as 9 and 10 were seeing therapists for anger and depression. Division and strife existed in their extended families, divorcing the entire family from cherished traditions. Many were losing the homes they had raised their children in. I think in particular of two women who had each been married more than 30 years and grieved the fact that no longer would their children and grandchildren be coming home to the only home they had ever known. As the younger women looked for work, dismay engulfed them as they ran into limited opportunities due to their lack of experience and education and having to leave their young children in daycare for the first time. Men were enrolled in anger management classes. Loneliness, money worries, feuds ignited by lawyers, and fears of the future kept them awake at night and drove them to doctors for antidepressants. They had the haunted look of refugees as everything normal and good in their lives was being blown to pieces. No wonder God emphatically declares in Mal. 2:16, that He hates divorce. Driving home after each session, I, too, came to hate it, and I wept for their pain and loss.

Precious Souls at Stake

But an even greater casualty is occurring than what meets the eye. In this marital war zone, the peace and power that comes from prayer is silenced. The confident, calm, reassuring presence of a life of hope and faith disappears. In the course of reconciling with David, I have come to realize that the loss of prayer, faith, and hope for our children is no small thing. I believe that our prayers are the most powerful weapons and defense for our children regarding their spiritual, emotional, and relational needs. As God brought healing to my wounded soul and marriage, I felt a keen loss of the years the swarming locusts had eaten away due to my sin (see Joel 2:25). I began to see clearly the enormous hole my spiritual and matrimonial mutiny had created in our home. It was like witnessing the aftermath of a flood or an earthquake. If I added up the years that encompassed my affair, my separation, and divorce, and especially the first year of reconciliation, I saw five years of pain and grief that had drawn my focus inward, leaving no room or energy for eternal matters. Five years lost in which I had failed to engage God regarding the souls of my children! In the midst of a fallen world that surrounds our children with temptation, danger, and evil we cannot afford such apostasy. For it is out of daily prayer that the pillars of faith and hope grow strong for our children, and this is what they see and what they want and ultimately what they reach for. If we are not standing in the gap, holding these lifelines out to them through a righteous life of prayer and presence that links them with the God who can save them, someone or something else will lure them.

While I was writing this chapter, our son Ryan called me from Las Vegas. In the course of our conversation, he said, "Mom, this past month something has clicked, something's gone on I can't explain. You know I haven't been living right. I've been depressed, I've been drinking and doing things I knew were not right. But a week ago I woke up and said to myself, *I am going to change.* Since then, I haven't touched a drink; I look forward to each day and—I am happy!" I hung up, and my love for our awesome God welled up in my heart as the tears rolled down my face. I knew what was happening even if Ryan could not find the words to express it: God was beginning to move in his life! And again, God jerked me upright, reminding me that this is what it's all about. This is what we stand to lose if we do not walk God's way. This is what we and our children risk losing if we persist in holding on to perversity while we willfully pursue our own happiness.

Could God save our children without my prayers? Certainly. He can and does! But I don't want to get to the end of my days prayerless and see my children's lives unchanged and wonder with untold regret, *What if? What might have been had I remained faithful and prayerful?*

Ryan has since found a church he loves, and he attends every week. His roommate started attending with him also. Two weeks ago Ryan called from Borders and asked his father what kind of Bible he should buy. There's no greater joy than this!

Passing the Torch

Joseph, from our earlier story, was not alone in his faithfulness to God. Before and after him were giants of the faith, such as Abraham, Isaac, Jacob, and then Moses. All of these men walked the line, stood in the gap, held onto their integrity and, in doing so, became a link in the fulfillment of God's promises to their own children and to an entire nation. The day the children of Israel crossed the River Jordan into the Promised Land, none of these men were there to witness it. They died never seeing the fulfillment of the promises God had given them. Yet they died, not in despair, but in hope (see Heb. 11:13). William Barclay wrote, "Our hopes may never be realized, but we must live in such a way that we will hasten their coming."[1]

Thousands of years later came another giant: Oswald Chambers. He, too, was a man known for his faithfulness, for having walked the line, for standing in the gap against all odds. Included in his biography was a journal entry dated February 16, 1907:

I want to tell you a growing conviction in me, and that is that as we obey the leadings of the Spirit of God, we enable God to answer the prayers of other people. I mean that our lives, my life, is the answer to someone's prayer prayed perhaps centuries ago. . . . I have the unspeakable knowledge that my life is the answer to prayers, and that God is blessing me and making me a blessing entirely of His sovereign grace and nothing to do with my merits . . . that is the great message to my heart these months.[2]

Many decades later came another giant of the faith: Rosella Johnson, my maternal grandmother. One day I will write a book about this great lady—if I can get over my sense of inadequacy to do her justice. Grandma's husband, Jerome, was an abusive and violent alcoholic who beat her and the children. When my mother was eight, she witnessed her father push her mother off their high porch, landing on her and breaking her back. One Christmas, Grandma had woven enough rugs so that she could sell them and buy each of the children ice skates, their only gift. Jerome gathered the gifts on Christmas Day and burned them in a bonfire outdoors.

Grandma gave her life to Christ early in the marriage, which only increased Jerome's abuse. Often, in the dead of a Pennsylvania winter, having hauled her children two miles to church on sleds, she would return home only to be locked out of the house. They had no choice but to sleep in the barn the entire night. If anyone had a right to divorce, my grandmother did. One day, as my aunt was sifting through some old legal papers, she discovered a document of divorce drawn up decades ago. When she asked my grandmother why she never went through with it, her only reply was, "God wouldn't let me."

Through all her adversity, prayer and her faith in the sovereignty of God kept her standing faithfully in the gap. My mother tells me that Grandmother could be heard praying under the porch, in the barn, in the attic. She prayed for her abusive husband, for her children, her church, her neighbors, future grandchildren. When she died at 90, here is part of her legacy. Not what might have been, but what *was:*

- All four children are saved and in the church today—one a retired minister. All four have celebrated 50-plus years of marriage. Her four children stopped the cycle of abuse and alcoholism that had been rampant in Grandfather's family.

- Almost all 16 grandchildren and several great-grandchildren are saved and active in their churches. Some are pastors, professors at Christian colleges, pastors' wives, teachers, doctors, Christian musicians, and writers.

- Grandmother was certain that Jerome made it to heaven. At 44, while away on one of his trips, Jerome died of heart failure due to alcoholism. A man in the hotel room beside Jerome's reported that throughout the night he heard a man who seemed to be "groaning and praying." It made sense. They found Jerome on his knees by his bedside with a Bible opened before him. A smile as wide as Texas could not be removed from his face.

I am not at all implying that we should stay in an abusive relationship, but many of us give up on our marriages where there is no hint of abuse but have other struggles that pale in comparison to what my grandmother faced. Grandma had a childlike faith in her Heavenly Father. He would either make a way through or there would be no way made at all—by her or anyone else. Through it all, she never failed to walk and not faint when it came to intercessory prayer.

Two years ago when she died, I got many of her books. What I found in her books firmly cemented the belief of how important it is to remain faithful and stand in the gap with intercessory prayer. Tucked away in many of them are single index cards—prayer cards—with one name on it and sometimes the date. These held the names of siblings, aunts, uncles, cousins, her church friends, and then one day, my name: Lyndell Hetrick. Hetrick was my maiden name. The card, yellowed and stained, had been tucked away with prayer more than 33 years earlier. Were Grandma's prayers key in leading me back home to God? Were her prayers a force behind the miracle that is now my marriage—how out of ruin God resurrected a broken life and marriage and now blesses our lives in immeasurable ways? I can only echo Oswald Chambers: I have a growing conviction, an unspeakable knowledge, that my life is the answer to someone's prayers centuries ago, decades ago, weeks ago. Someone who stayed or stays in the race; someone who stood or stands in the gap; who saw or sees himself or herself as a key in the fulfillment of God's promises for my life. Yes. I am absolutely convinced that I am reaping today what the faithful have sown. I can respond only with deep gratitude and do likewise as I reach out and take the torch.

How is it that Abraham was able to offer up Isaac as a sacrifice? I believe it's because God had given him the big picture long before, "Go forth from your country . . . from your father's house, to the land which I will show you; and I will make you a great nation, and I will bless you, and make your name great . . . and in you all the families of the earth will be blessed" (Gen. 12:1-3, NASB). It would be through Isaac that this big picture would be fulfilled. When God called Abraham to prepare Isaac as a sacrifice, Abraham quickly obeyed. Even though what he was commanded to do was beyond irrational, Abraham had to sense greatly that his obedience was a link to the fulfillment of God's big picture, not only for his family but for an entire nation. Past experiences had taught him that God *always* provides and keeps His promises.

Sometimes it makes no sense at all to remain in

our marriages. It certainly did not for my grandmother, and many told her so. But see what God accomplished because *one person* stood unshakably on the rock of God's promises in the midst of evil. See what Abraham accomplished even though he was surrounded by an idolatrous nation and family. The one common denominator for both is the belief that life was meant to be bigger than one man's or one woman's desires. Therefore, something grand was at stake and God was bigger than any mountain they faced, and He will always provide.

God has not changed. He is a God who has a big picture in mind for every family, even if just one light shines for Him. In fact, we can claim the big-picture promise He gave Abraham. To paraphrase Gen. 12:1-3: "Leave your idolatrous ways and separate yourself from all forms of ungodly guidance. Enter into your marriage and allow Me to lead you. I will give you a wonderful family, and I will give you a great legacy. Because of your obedience, I will never fail to bless your descendants."

This is exactly what God is doing in my family. After I reconciled with David, He began to give me the big picture. As my soul began to rediscover all the good things that had died within me, I was gripped with a burden for the salvation of our children. Feeling the need to make up for lost time, I began to pray daily and fervently for their souls. As God began to answer prayer, He began to restore to me the missing years devoured by the locusts of sin; He began to show me what I had been missing. And each time He adds to the picture it becomes bigger, for He strengthens the message of what is at stake if we drop out of the race. Reading the following journal entries, I hope you, too, will get the picture:

December 19, 2005

> *Two nights ago Ryan called and asked if I would pray for Christy, his girlfriend: "Mom, she is so lost. She tried to commit suicide yesterday. I know you pray, and I know that God hears you. I need you to pray for her because I don't know how else to help her."*

February 6, 2006

> *As we drove home from church today my cell phone rings and Jackie (our youngest) was sobbing on the other end: "When are you coming home? I need to talk to you." Arriving home, we discovered that she and her boyfriend had broken up. What gripped her with fear was the realization that this has been her pattern in all her relationships. At 23, she could not hold down a relationship and was afraid to try. In the course of David and I talking with her, we led her to the source of the real problem, which was trying to establish significant relationships while her primary relationship with God is broken. For the first time*

in a long time, as we talked about her need for Christ, a light came on in her eyes. She leaned forward, hungry for the truth and seeming to realize that where she was in her relationship with her boyfriend was secondary to where she was with God. Several minutes later, we were kneeling before God—Jackie and David and I—listening to Jackie invite Jesus into her heart, into her "broken, messed up life" with a mature earnestness that had never been present before.

Recently our oldest son, Chad, who will receive a degree in theology next month, wrote a paper about our journey as a family. Here is a portion of his paper that continues to broaden God's big picture for our family:

There are certain moments that radically change our lives. One such moment occurred while I was in the navy, stationed in Japan. I received an e-mail from my mom and dad saying they were divorcing due to my mom having an affair. My semi-cozy world as a pastor's kid on vacation from God for the past 10 years, secure in the knowledge that his parents are still "there" and that I, the prodigal son, could return home one day to receive blessings, shattered in that moment. What does a prodigal son do when he has squandered away his life and then realizes that there is no home for him to return to? I did what my childhood had taught me and cried out for God's mercy and hoped that God would "remember" us. Wondrously, He did.

It was a long, hard road. However, His "remembrance" of us came to fruition piece by piece. Returning from Japan, I was caught between two dueling parents and three siblings taking sides. I witnessed more than a son ever expects to witness. When I drove my sobbing father home one evening after trying to console him and then called my mother to cuss her out for putting him (and me) in this position, I felt like I was staring at a raging Red Sea with attackers surrounding me on all sides. I wondered if God would ever remember us or if He even existed. And then the sea began to part.

What I can only call miracles began to take place. My mother and father began to talk again. Bridges that I thought were long burned and destroyed were being mended and healed. And the sea finally parted when on Valentine's Day 2003, with tears streaming down my face, I watched two broken people being completely restored and remade by the hand of God as they said to one another, "I do." In that holy moment, I knew within my heart of hearts that if God could restore them, He could restore me.

Shortly after, I recommitted my life to Christ and the call to full-time ministry was renewed once again. I since have been blessed with a wonderful Christian wife and two sons. In the winter of 2006 I will graduate with a degree in theology and head to seminary to pursue ordination. Every chance I get to preach, I love to tell the story of how God is still the God who brings people out of bondage and across the rough waters of life. And every time I see my parents together, I am grateful for their obedience and for God's faithfulness, for it reached out and set this once prodigal son on the road toward home.

When we are in an adulterous relationship, the curtain on the big picture is closed. To remain in it is to never see what's behind the curtain. If Jesus had acted on His feelings and laid down His cross, we would not have seen what was behind the veil. We would not be reaping today the blessings of God's big picture of salvation for all people. The effects of such a choice would ripple through every generation.

On a smaller scale, that is our fate and the legacy we leave when we lay down our cross by committing adultery and leaving our spouse for another. When we indulge our feelings and arrogantly claim our rights, our world shrinks to accommodate one person: me. Living in our shrunken world, God's blessings shrink to nothing. Lysa TerKeurst wrote, "We will never experience the radical blessings God has in store for us without radical obedience."[3] I believe with all my heart that the locusts would have won had David and I remained apart. Instead, what a blessing and great joy it has been to watch an awesome God at work in our children's lives.

Do you have a dream for your family? Do you have a dream of the kind of legacy you want to leave? Has God given you the big picture He has designed just for you and your family? If not, simply ask Him for it. He will burn it into your soul. But first, two things must occur:

- You must commit to radical obedience that brings radical blessings. Look at the areas of your life where you are not obeying God. Until we are walking upright in the land God has given us, He will not show us new land to walk upon. List below areas where you are engaging in disobedience that is obscuring God's big picture:

- We cannot rewrite God's Word or put a spin on it to suit our desires. We are in treacherous territory when we convince ourselves that sin is God's will. If you are living that lie, ask for forgiveness and resolve to live in truth.

12

Restoring the Vision of God's Glory

*T*he words *idolatry* and *adultery* sound similar, don't they? And they are similar, because when one engages in adultery, he or she is also engaging in idolatry— bowing before a false god. Idolatry is as old as Adam and Eve, and it is what incurred God's greatest wrath upon the Israelites. Ezekiel 8 shows us a day in the life of idolaters. God's commentary and His reaction toward the idolaters of Ezekiel's day is what we can expect when we engage in idolatrous behavior.

While the prophet Ezekiel and other Israelites are in Babylonian captivity, Ezekiel is transported in a vision to the Jerusalem Temple to see the abominations that are grieving God—idol worship, spirit worship, nature worship, and sun worship. At the north gate of the Temple, Ezekiel sees the first abomination—God's people worshiping the Canaanite fertility goddess, also known as the idol of jealousy. As Ezekiel was taking it in, God begins His narrative, "Son of man, do you see what they are doing, the great abominations which the house of Israel are committing here, so that I would be far from My sanctuary? But yet you will see still greater abominations" (v. 6, NASB). Moving Ezekiel to another spot, the *greater abomination* was the sight of 70 elders of the house of Israel holding incense in their hands and worshiping idols carved in the wall featuring every form of creeping thing, beast, and detestable things. As Ezekiel takes in this abominable scene, God says, "Son of man, do you see what the elders of the house of Israel are committing in the dark, each man in the room of his carved images? For they say, 'The LORD does not see us; the LORD has forsaken the land'" (v. 12, NASB). And he finished, "Yet you will see still greater abominations which they are committing" (v. 13, NASB). Whisked to another gate, "Behold, women were sitting there weeping for Tammuz" (v. 14, NASB) to bring rain and vegetation to their parched land, and they worshiped this Babylonian god of nature with acts of base immorality. But God was not finished. The final insult God wanted Ezekiel to see was a picture of 25 men who had deliberately turned their backs to the Temple, faced the east, and prostrated themselves toward the sun. To which God said, "Do you see this, son of man? . . . Behold, they are putting the twig to their nose" (v. 17), which is a Hebrew idiom for an insulting gesture (see vv. 3-17, NASB).

The Tragic Loss of Glory

I can only imagine what Ezekiel would see if he looked into the windows of our churches today. Would he be shocked to see the spirits of jealousy, pride, and greed? Would he be shocked at the rampant immorality that is sweeping through our churches today? Probably not. We are not much different from the worshipers of his day who engaged in idolatry. We are just better at hiding it. We multitask in the church so effectively that we can hide from everyone else what only God sees. But when God calls our bluff for living like the inside of the cup is clean when it isn't, we experience the same tragedy that the idolaters of Ezekiel's day experienced. We are robbed of God's glory—which is the active, powerful, and loving presence of God.

After Ezekiel saw all the abominations that the people of God were committing that made a pretense of their worship, he next saw God's reaction: God's glory slowly departed from the Temple and from His people. In Ezek. 9:3 (NASB) we read, "Then the glory of the God of Israel went up from the cherub on which it had been, to the threshold of the temple." In 10:18-19 (NASB) we read, "Then the glory of the LORD departed from the threshold of the temple and stood over the cherubim. When the cherubim departed, they . . . stood still at the entrance of the east gate of the LORD's house, and the glory of the God of Israel hovered over them." Then in 11:23 (NASB) we read, "The glory of the LORD went up from the midst of the city and stood over the mountain which is east of the city." From the cherubim to the threshold to the east gate the Lord slowly departed. At the final stage of His departure, His glory rested on the Mount of Olives. Interestingly, it was on this same mountain that Jesus stood and wept over Jerusalem and from which He ascended into heaven.

The first time I read this account in Ezekiel of the Lord's glory slowly departing from His people, I wept. If we ever grasp the glory of the Lord in our lives, we will discover that it is a tragic thing to lose.

Today, we look full into the face of glory in the person of Jesus Christ. All the glory of God revealed in the Old Testament resides in Him. And the wonder of wonders is that this King of Glory would deign to stoop and knock at our heart's door desiring entrance so that He can dine with us (Rev. 3:20) and make His home in us (John 14:23). In a later vision, Ezekiel saw the glory of the Lord return to the millennial Temple, making the earth shine. It was a foreshadowing of what occurs when God descends into our bodies, His temple, with all the fullness of the Godhead. The temple in which God shines today is our hearts, His sanctuary. In broken vessels this treasure now resides. How amazing that *we* become the temple of the living God!

The unparalleled honor of being the temple where the glory of the living God now longs to dwell stabbed and thrilled my soul three years after David and I reconciled. I was gripped as never before with the magnitude of my adulterous ways against God. I finally understood why an immoral act is the only sin that is a sin against one's own body. I saw the powerful connection between the departure of God's glory from the Temple in Ezekiel's day and why God's glory departed from me the day I bowed to the god of adultery. I saw how I grieved Him.

Pretending at Church

The problem with trying to *carry on* in our worship of God and in our service to Him when His glory has departed not only makes our worship a sham but also leaves our hearts always longing for *something* that we can't quite identify. Though we are Christians, we are still hungry and unfulfilled, leaving us to ask, *Where is the joy of our salvation?*

Unable to find answers, we begin to follow the Pharisees among us who say, "You must act like this; look like that; think like us; serve like this" in order to be a faithful follower of Jesus, which translates to *"doing must bring about the joy of my salvation."* So we teach Sunday School, serve on committees, join the evangelism team, and teach Bible studies. But before long we feel trapped and tired of "should of, ought to, have to, need to." Yet we are also aware that we can't quit, for we are now held hostage by the gilded image we have created. So we work harder to maintain the image in order to cover up what is festering inside, unable to disclose them for fear of being rejected or misunderstood.

When asked, "How are you?" you respond with a smile and say, "Just fine," when in reality you are empty inside and are wondering, *Is this what it's all about?*

Dallas Willard, one of the premier theological scholars of our day, has pegged it well. When asked about today's typical Christian, he said:

> Generally, what I find is that the ordinary people that come to church are basically running their lives on their own. . . . They believe there is a God and they need to check in with Him. But they don't have any sense that He is an active agent in their lives. As a result, they don't become disciples of Jesus Christ. They consume His

merits and the services of the church. . . . But discipleship is not an essential part of Christianity today. When you don't have character transformation in a large number of your people, then when something happens, everything flies apart and you have people acting in the most ungodly ways imaginable.[1]

When the difficulties of life and temptation storm the lives and marriages of such people they collapse like a house built on sinking sand—like ours did. In 1998, my life mirrored Willard's final comment. Having a "religion" without transformation when difficulties hit, my life flew apart and I reacted in the most ungodly of ways. I was clueless as to how my behavior was greatly damaging my body, God's temple, but also His Body, the Church.

There is no question that my adultery made public hurt the Body of Christ, but I had hurt the Body before that. Having lacked the real thing, I became skilled at creating a hollow shell of the real thing among the family of God. For 18 months, my entire life was a lie. I was engaged in an extramarital affair while engaged in the affairs of the church. I was a master at projecting the image of the happy Christian in a happy marriage. We may fool others, but there is never a moment when we fool God.

One day God called my bluff, and my hollow shell crumbled. When what appears to be a strong,

Christian marriage buckles due to immorality, it threatens the faith of others. Only God knows the depth of disillusionment my fall created in the lives of fellow believers.

I have discovered that polishing the outward marks of Christianity while hiding an idolatrous heart from God and His people is sheer folly. When we live as if the inside of the cup is clean when it isn't, we will have a sense that God has forsaken us. The more deceptive the charade becomes, the further God's glory retreats.

When we ignore what is happening and continue to play the game of church, we risk becoming a dropout in God's kingdom and taking others with us. We never experience the abundant life that Christ died to give us. When life falls apart, we act in ungodly ways.

What's Missing?

Why is ungodly, immoral behavior happening at such an alarming rate among Christians? Did we not get saved? Can we not point to the day we repented? Many of us can. Yet we must think that repentance is not enough. The ultimate goal of repentance is to transform our hearts and character—not just save us from hell—and it takes a lifetime. Repentance simply opens the door to let the light in. The act of repentance in our hearts is like flipping on the light switch in a cluttered museum. With the first burst of light it is impossible to see everything at once that has been in the dark collecting dust. It is only as we take time, move about, touch things, peer under things, move things to discover other things that we see what we want to keep or throw away.

This is exactly what Jesus does when we open our hearts to Him. To become transformed, we must be searched and rescued by God. He enters with His purifying light and searches out every dusty nook and cranny of our hearts with one purpose in mind—to rescue our flesh and spirit from the layers of deceit and filth that have hindered our walk, weighed us down, and robbed us of the joy of our salvation.

Because we fear such scrutiny by God, we dodge Him and try to hide our hearts from Him. We don't want God up-close and personal, because He may not like what He sees and therefore not like us. However, without such transparency there can be no transformation of heart and character. We need repentance that leads to transparency that leads to transformation of heart that leads to godly character.

Grace Transforms Our Hearts

I have come to believe that many of the moral problems Christians struggle with today are because we have diminished the need for grace. Our behavior says, "Thank you, Grace, for aiding in my salvation, but I can take it from here."

Without God's grace in our hearts, we are all vulnerable to being ensnared by the roots of bitterness, hopelessness, and immorality. Without grace we try to transform ourselves from the outside in. All our focus is placed on cleaning the outside of the cup rather than the inside. We place more emphasis on *doing* rather than on *being*. Thus, we see faces untouched by joy because we always fail to measure up. We see shriveled faces that are judgmental, which brings division and isolation. Not seeing grace-filled faces of compassion and mercy, people isolate themselves from the much-needed prayer, encouragement, and healing they need. In isolation, they are overcome by temptation and trade their birthright for pursuits that satisfy the flesh. In so doing, they exchange the glory of God for shame.

When Jesus descends into our hearts, He brings the glory of His grace and truth. John said that "for of his fullness we have all received, and grace upon grace" (John 1:16, NASB). This literally means grace piled upon grace throughout the experiences of our Christian life. When God's truth uncovers the dirt in our earthly temples, His endless grace follows behind to cover with love and mercy. To truly grasp this amazing process in our lives is to humbly echo Paul who claimed he gloried only in the cross of Christ—for without the Cross there would be no grace (see Gal. 6:14). Grace is what embraces us and enables us to embrace others in spite of our own spots. It is love and acceptance from God and to one another because we have been washed by the blood of the Lamb. We did not earn grace, Christ earned it for us. Therefore, we do not expect others to measure up in order to earn it from us. We did not deserve it, but God gave it as a gift. He knew we could never be obedient to such a command unless we were constantly showered with His grace.

Grace in Action Transforms Others

In one of my favorite movies, *Seabiscuit*, there is one particular scene that gives us a picture of grace in action. A wealthy car dealer, Charles Howard, decides to enter the world of horseracing. Needing a trainer, a horse, and a jockey, he hires Tom Smith, a has-been trainer, to find the horse and jockey. Tom finds Seabiscuit, a has-been racehorse, and Red, a has-been, hardened, and bitter jockey. A more unlikely crew could not be found in all of horseracing at the time, but to the surprise of all, Seabiscuit begins to win big. Riding the wave of a six-win streak, they enter a high stakes race where Seabiscuit was favored to win—and he almost did. Thinking he had it in the bag, Red eased up on the reins and was blindsided by another horse and rider. Overtaking Seabiscuit, they win by a nose. Tom Smith was livid. Cornering Red in the barracks afterward, he berated Red for slacking off while a rider was flanking him on the left. Red interrupts his tirade and yells that he couldn't see him. Realizing what Red just revealed, Tom storms out and finds Charles, "He lied to us! He can't see! He's *blind* in his left eye!" A shocked silence hung between them as both took in the ramifications of such news. Then Tom says, "What do you want to do with him?" Since Red had failed to reveal that he was half blind, it naturally warranted the end of his career. Instead, Charles walks up to Tom, places a hand on each shoulder, and with a smile that was grace-filled said, "You don't throw a whole life away just because it's banged up a little." Such an affirmation removed the hardness and healed Red's bitterness, allowing him to stand tall once again.

This is the same picture of grace we see in Jeremiah when God likens himself to a potter (see Jer. 18:1-6). If you've ever seen a potter at work, you will notice a pile of rubble nearby. Into this pile the potter tosses the hopeless pieces—pieces so marred that it would be a waste of time to keep working on them. But God is not an ordinary potter. There is no pile of rubble nearby. When God searches out our deceitful heart and finds it badly marred by sin, even though we had projected an image that said we were whole, instead of tossing us aside as hopeless, He draws us close and says, "Don't worry. I don't throw a whole life away just because it's banged up a little." And unlike Charles, whose grace toward Red is finite, God's grace to us is infinite and can plummet to the deepest depths of our souls to touch and heal whatever is wounded and stained within.

Without this kind of grace to cover the truth about ourselves, we cannot bare our untidy souls to God, nor can we bear what we bare. When I confessed my sins that day on the kitchen floor, it was God's truth that brought my sin into the light, and I saw that I, indeed, was a sinner, an adulterer in need of forgiveness. It was God's grace that kept me from collapsing under the weight of such knowledge. God's grace allowed me to stand in my pain and not run from it. Little did I know that was just the beginning of God's work of truth and grace in my life. After my divorce, He began to uncover more than I ever wanted to know. I had a choice each time I was faced with a new truth: I could stop short of grace by running away from the truth and deny it, or I could allow His truth and grace to plummet to the deepest depths of my soul and do its healing and cleansing work, for only God knows the depth of our deceitfulness. Thankfully, I chose to cry out, "Lord, come! Whatever it takes, clean up my act—inside and out!" Though it was painful, He began to root out the bitterness, the lust, the selfishness, the pride, the self-righteousness; He healed the shame, the sorrow, the deep wounds, the painful memories. In the process, the joy of my salvation was restored; He returned in all His glory, bringing a sweet and active presence unlike I have ever known. So much so that I continue to give Him more of me, for I hunger for more of Him.

Having allowed grace and truth to do its work, I now realize what I had been missing all along! I had created a God who was comfortable sharing His glory with all the other idols in my heart. I had created a God that did not expect me to be holy and therefore made allowances for my humanness. I had created a God who overlooked the impurity of my heart because of all the sacrifices I made for Him in the church. Having failed to submit to the Spirit's truth, whose job is to break down every idol and cast out every foe, and having failed to cling to God's grace that removes the shame, I had forfeited God's glory— His favor and active presence in my life. No wonder I had plodded through most of my Christian life sensing that God was hovering far away, watching me uncaringly from a distance.

Grace Transforms Us into Grace-Full People

When we allow God's infinite grace to plummet to the deepest depths of our souls and touch and heal whatever is wounded and marred within, we can't help but be grace-full people in the Body of Christ— and we desperately need them. We need wounded healers restored by grace who drop their stones and do not walk away from the spots and wrinkles. When we are on the receiving end of grace, when we know that we don't deserve it, we are in our glory—God's glory. God comes into our midst and we are set free to unload our hearts and receive God's truth.

My mother is a wonderful example of a person full of grace. If anyone had a right to be angry and bitter and still haunted by her abusive past, she did. It has taken her years to open her heart to the glory of truth and grace, but she will tell you that the commitment to truth and the receiving of grace has healed her deepest wounds and set her free. As a result, grace was on her face and in her response the day I confessed to her that I had committed adultery. It was the hardest and yet most glorious moment I have ever encountered.

My mother sat across the table from me. With tears of brokenness, I poured out the truth of what I had done. I held nothing back. I took full blame. This went on for several minutes while my mother sat silently and motionless. At one point, she cupped her hand over her mouth and chin and leaned her elbow on the table, supporting her head and suddenly looking weary. Finally, emotionally spent, I stopped talking, for I had nothing left to say. For several seconds she didn't move. A heavy silence hung between us. Then, without a word, she slowly got up, walked around the table, and took me into her arms. There she held and rocked me as we both wept.

I had always believed in my mother's love for me, but that day, her faithful, loving response to an unfaithful daughter brought a deep *knowing* of her love that I will never doubt again. In her faithful, loving response we shared in the glory of God's loving presence, His healing grace, and His liberating truth. The confession of my sin to a grace-full, righteous woman enabled the healing work to begin.

If a woman in my church, whom I respected, had approached me years ago as I struggled in my marriage and asked, "Lyndell, how is your marriage? Are you happy in it? Is your relationship honoring God?" I would have burst into tears, not only because of the subject but because she dared and cared enough to wade that deeply into me—inviting truth and giving grace. I like to think had that occurred we could have turned the tide of an unhappy marriage away from the fatal shore of adultery.

But the stories we are hearing tell us that many in the Body of Christ are silent in their struggles and suffering alone. When fallible, imperfect humans project a picture of perfection, it can be disheartening to those who struggle in their own imperfection. Needing an atmosphere of truth and grace, they instead feel judgment and condemnation, which silences them. Thus, they conform by mirroring the perfect stories they see and yet cry, "Am I the only one struggling here? Is everyone perfect except me?"

However, something of great magnitude is missing when we are silent. If we are not free to tell our stories, then God's story is absent in the church. If we are not telling our stories of brokenness as God directs, then we are not telling God's story of deliverance. If we can't tell of our bondage and God's deliverance, then how will others be given the hope that God could do the same for them? Conversely, if we can't share that we *are* in bondage, then how can we ever receive encouragement and prayer along with the healing that is promised when we confess our sins one to another? Put simply, if we are not sharing our stories, we are not sharing in God's glory. To create the illusion that we are infallible, perfect human beings who have our act together apart from grace and truth is to enable Satan, shut out the manifestations of God's glory, and silence our testimonies. Thus, the silenced and the suffering slowly depart from God and the church; first in their hearts, then from each other, and finally in their behavior.

We need grace-full Christians who have experienced amazing grace in the midst of great personal failure to tell their stories so that God's story can be told. We need the voices and touches of wounded healers among us. Transparent on the inside, they are transparent on the outside. They are active participants in allowing God to transform their own lives and in helping others seek transformation. They are couples who are willing to reveal the struggles and failures as well as the victories, humble couples whose marriages reflect complete dependence on God because they've been to the brink and back. Such couples are not afraid to hear the truth, and they are not stingy with grace, for they can honestly declare, "There but for the grace of God go I."

This is genuine Christian community at its best: "a healing community not because wounds are cured and pains are alleviated, but because wounds and pains become openings or occasions for a new vision. Mutual confession then becomes a mutual deepening of hope, and sharing weakness becomes a reminder to one and all of the coming strength."[2]

I have talked a lot in this book about how my false concept of God's love for me hindered me from having a deep and abiding relationship with Christ. Adultery changed all that. I finally came to understand that where sin abounds, grace abounds all the more. Sadly, I had to commit a gross act of sin for that knowledge to light a fire in my soul. Had I just once grasped that the Creator of the universe, the *living God*, wanted to dwell in my heart as His temple, then grace would have been elevated to its transforming height. To now have the knowledge of the glory of His grace radiate in this earthly, banged-up temple is to walk with my head held high as a daughter of the King. The most essential thing in keeping God's glory or in restoring it is to surrender to God's truth and humbly receive His grace each day. When we clearly see our need for grace, we can genuinely extend it to others.

For years, I claimed to be obedient to God, yet knew nothing of real obedience. The obedience I exercised focused more on *doing* rather than *being.* Doing was easy—go to church, pay tithe, don't seek revenge, read the Bible and pray, teach Sunday School, lead a Bible study, support the programs of the church, and the list goes on and on, but when my marriage ended, so did the duties, and God had my attention. I was guilty of the words in Isaiah: "This people draw near with their words, and honor Me with their lip service, but they remove their hearts from Me, and their reverence for Me consists of tradition learned by rote" (Isa. 29:13, NASB). All the "doings" of my life had not been a result of my obedience at all. In fact, I had been disobedient where it counted most—my inner being.

Real obedience will put us in desperate need of grace. C. S. Lewis said, "No man knows how bad he really is till he has tried very hard to be good."[3] When Jesus calls us to be perfected in holiness in our inner and outer beings, the first thing we see is what He wants us to see: We can't do it without grace.

Sick of playing church and longing to experience what it is like to have the Spirit of Christ operating fully in my life, I have made three vows before God:

- To be radical about inner purity
- To practice radical obedience to what He reveals

- To embrace His truth as my reality

Jesus minced no words when it came to people who did good works with impure hearts:

> Woe to you, scribes and Pharisees, hypocrites! For you clean the outside of the cup and of the dish, but inside they are full of robbery and self-indulgence . . . Clean the inside of the cup and of the dish, so that the outside of it may become clean also. . . . For you are like whitewashed tombs which on the outside appear beautiful, but inside they are full of dead men's bones and all uncleanness *(Matt. 23:25-27, NASB)*.

When it comes to purity of heart, there are no gray areas. The inside of the cup and dish are either clean or they are not. Maintaining moral purity is necessary to maintain a pure heart. To be pure morally in marriage, you must:

- Cast out unholy affections and release desires and longings that entice us
- Take control over unholy and lustful thoughts
- Refuse to allow yourself to imagine liaisons with someone other than your spouse
- Forbid thoughts that allow you to imagine a future with someone better

When you commit to transform your inner self, your outer self will be transformed as well, for your eyes will be opened to realities you may have denied:

- You will begin to see that much of the strife

and tension that existed in your marriage was a result of the unholy activity you harbored in your mind.

- You will see that compromising your thoughts leads to placing yourself in compromising situations.

- You will see that excusing your thought life because it doesn't hurt anyone leads to excusing *behavior* as long as it doesn't hurt anyone.

- You will see that letting your thoughts become impure will cause you to be tempted to yield to the flesh.

- You will see that your spouse looked undesirable because a fantasy about someone else had become more desirable.

Sin that separates us from God and others begins in our thoughts. God asks for our thoughts in order to cleanse and heal them. It is grace that invites us to tell God the truth about our ugly thoughts. When we entertain forbidden thoughts, it leads to careless thinking and careless living, thus blinding us to the truth that our marriage and our relationship with God suffered or ended because we were first unfaithful in our thoughts.

Once we commit to purity of heart and mind, we can strive to be obedient to everything God reveals. Andrew Murray knew this well. He writes:

When we humbly ask Him to teach us how

to obey God in everything, He asks us if we are ready to pay the price: it is to entirely and utterly deny self. It is to give up our will, our life, even unto death. . . . Unless we take the vow of absolute obedience as we enter this class in Christ's school, it will be impossible to make any real progress.[4]

To be transformed will require you to say no to anyone, anything, or any activity that dirties the inside of the cup. Once you invite Him to be up-close and personal, be prepared for Him to point out lying, cheating, flirting, self-centeredness, selfish ambitions, unforgiving attitudes, pride, uncontrolled anger, cop-out responses such as "That's just the way I am" or "We're just friends," shameful computer activity, entertainment that glorifies immorality or sex or nudity, and the places you go. In other words, He will turn your complacent world upside down. He knows it is the only way you will get the *dead men's bones,* referred to in Matt. 23, out of your heart so that you may truly live. We can hide nothing from God.

God wants us to embrace His truth as our reality. When He begins to uncover falsehoods and replace them with truth, remember He gives us His grace. We may squirm, but we need not hide in shame, deny it with pride, run from it in fear. Rather, we embrace the reality by agreeing with God, "Yes, Lord. This is true about me. Always has been. I see that your desire is to make me holy and righteous and that this must be

confessed and it must go. I want to be all you want
me to be and to walk in complete obedience. I yield
to your truth and will make the adjustment I need to
make to bring my life into alignment with the truth
you have revealed."

In so doing, you will experience His love and a
deeply intimate relationship with Him. It allows a
better understanding of 1 John 1:7, "But if we walk in
the light as he is in the light, we have fellowship with
one another, and the blood of Jesus, his Son, purifies
us from all sin."

So let me ask you:

- Do you long to allow God to be up-close and
  personal and transform you? Are you willing to
  commit to inner purity? If so, write your vow
  to God.

- Are you willing to be radically obedient to
  what God reveals to you? Are you willing to say
  no to anyone, anything, or any activity that
  might compromise your vow to inner and outer purity?

- Are you willing to embrace God's truth as the
  only reality for your life? If so, write out your
  vow of commitment to live by God's truth in
  every area of your life.

- What have you learned about grace? How will
  your understanding of it aid you in your commitment to inner purity?

Now or Never: Promised Land or Wilderness?

I first met a woman I'll call Sara at a conference I attended. There were 200 in attendance, and we were divided into 20 small groups. It was the group leader's job to divide the small group into prayer partners. So for the three days of the conference, Sara and I were prayer partners.

We were instructed to first share with each other our passion—the message God had laid on our hearts to share with others through our writing and speaking. I told her that my passion was to help people in hurting marriages. I shared with her how love and respect had died in our marriage and when major challenges and tragedy struck simultaneously, our marriage crumbled under the weight. I went on to explain that my passion is to tell the story of an awesome God who has the power to redeem, restore, and rebuild broken lives and marriages, for He has since healed our marriage, even though it had ended in a bitter divorce.

My story touched a wounded place in Sara, and as she listened, tears streamed down her face. Grasping my hand, she said, "That is me too. That is where I am in my marriage; I no longer love my husband, and I don't know what to do." Sara had been married 18 years and was director of women's ministry in her church.

Later that night, Sara and I went to dinner with three other women. I was again asked to tell my story as to why I was attending the conference. I began my story, but this time I was nudged by the Holy Spirit, and I looked at Sara and said, "I neglected to tell you earlier today when we talked that I had an affair, and that is the real reason my marriage ended."

Sara was shocked. As I shared more about how God took a completely dead marriage and breathed life back into it, Sara's tears flowed once again. She was extremely quiet as we walked back to our hotel. As we rode the elevator to our rooms, we were delighted to discover our rooms were side-by-side on the same floor. Suddenly it became clear to me that God had orchestrated our meeting, and He wasn't done with this conversation.

I stood outside her door and asked if I could pray with her, but before I prayed I said, "Sara, God loves you so much that He arranged for us to meet today. Out of 200 people, He put us in the same group. He arranged for us to be prayer partners, and now your room is right next to mine. If God went to such great lengths to bring us together, don't you think He did it because He needed you to hear my story of reconciliation because He longs to perform the same miracle in your marriage?" I took her hands in mine and asked, "Is there someone else?" She began to sob. "Yes! Five months ago we met, and he offers everything that is lacking in my marriage—passion, love, someone who cares. Yet, like you said, if someone had told me a year ago I would be involved in an affair I would have laughed out loud. Here I am doing the very thing I said I would never do! Yet, I cannot imagine ever loving my husband again in the same way."

After I prayed with her, I walked into my room and was humbled to my knees. That night I was convinced as never before that God cares about our marriages. He passionately cares about the decisions we are making regarding them. I wanted for Sara to believe that God could redeem her marriage, restore love again, and rebuild her marriage in ways she never thought possible. How tragic it would be if she missed it! How tragic it would be if she turned away from what her marriage could be. God had brought her all the way to the doorstep that night. Her concerns were of gigantic proportions, yet they paled in comparison to a giant God when it comes to irreconcilable differences. God came to reconcile us with Him and with one another. But I know very well that it can be one of the hardest and most frightening things we are ever called to do.

The Call to the Promised Land

Reconciliation with David was the last thing I ever wanted. Like Sara, I was empty of feelings, desire, and hope. I could not believe that my happiness would be found in reconciling with David. I could not imagine us ever being intimate again. I could not imagine ever loving him again or being delighted with his presence. Both our actions over the past three years—from his discovery of my affair and his reaction to me telling him I did not love him anymore—had caused so much hurt that when we were in the same room a wall of pain stood between us. And it seemed impenetrable. A year after we were divorced, however, David wanted to reconcile. I answered with an emphatic no! God and I had an unspoken agreement that we wouldn't venture there or give it a second thought. I thought the Lord and I had agreed that it was over. Besides, I was in another relationship. Though I had turned to God, I was still very concerned about being happy, and I was convinced that remarriage to David would not make me happy. Little did I realize that God hated divorce because not only was He passionate about marriage, but He is also passionate about reconciliation. God had a hard time convincing me that He wanted me to tell David yes instead of no. He finally got through to me in a dramatic way.

It started with great unrest over my new relationship. Though I had no peace and felt that God was telling me to end it, I couldn't. I now see that I was simply afraid of being alone. My heart was still bruised over the affair and David's rejection, so I escaped into companionship. In the midst of my turmoil, David e-mailed me again—even after I had said no several times—and in essence said, "Let's try again." This time I went to my knees at my bedside, holding the printed e-mail in my hand, and prayed, *Lord, show me what to do. I am so full of fear and doubt. I don't see how it is possible for us to ever reconcile. But if that is what you want, you must reveal it to me in an unmistakable way.* Though I was in turmoil, I was determined to do what God wanted me to do. I knew that it was only through my obedience that I would be linked to God's greatest blessings for my life, which I greatly desired. Yet in my stubbornness, I was sure that His greatest blessing would not be found through reconciliation with David.

I was jerked awake at 5 A.M. the morning after that prayer by a man's loud voice. "Oh, that you had heeded My commandments. Then your peace would have been like a river, and your righteousness like the waves of the sea." I peered into the dark, certain that a man was standing in the corner of my room. The voice had spoken a scripture verse, but I did not know where to find it. Having a hard time believing that the Lord had actually spoken audibly to me, I grabbed my Bible from the nightstand and prayed a prayer that had never worked for me: *Lord, if that was really you, allow me to open my Bible to the page this verse is on.* I opened to the very page: Isa. 48:18, NKJV. Instantly, I knew why He had spoken those words.

Four years earlier I had underlined this verse when I broke off my affair for the first time. I even dated it. God had warned me then: "Obey me, and you will know peace; disobey and you will know no peace and only unhappiness." I had not obeyed, and as God said, I had no peace, plus I lost everything. God was clearly saying to me that morning, "I gave these words to you before when you were not at peace but you did not heed them. And look where it has left you, and you still have no peace. I give them to you again, and in doing so, I am giving you a second chance for my greatest blessings—peace, righteousness, and real joy." Somehow, I knew it would be my last chance—that I would be making the most tragic mistake of my life if I did not reconcile with David. That it would leave me wandering in a wilderness, restless and without peace, for the rest of my life.

The next day, though it was extremely painful, I ended the other relationship. I e-mailed David and told him I was willing to try again. When fear and doubt would consume me as I made preparations to move to where David was, I held fast to the words that had burned into my soul that morning, knowing that God had intervened in a mighty way to turn me toward the only path to true happiness. I knew, though I did not *feel* it, that I had received an unmistakable call to a brand-new land of promise that held the "milk and honey" of fulfilled hopes and dreams. Once there, He would heal our hearts, rebuild the ruins, and restore our marriage to complete wholeness.

Giants in the Promised Land

Holding on to that strong belief while I was still in Pennsylvania was one thing. Moving to St. Louis to reconcile with my estranged husband was another thing altogether. God had convinced me that I was to reconcile with David. Yet at the same time, I was aware of the seemingly impossible task that was before us. To bolster my confidence in God's power over the impossible, I had taken a book from my mother's shelf titled *Lord of the Impossible* by Lloyd John Ogilvie. This wonderful book did not fail me; in fact, if you are trying to reconcile and facing the impossible, I strongly recommend this book. However, upon arriving in St. Louis, I did what Ogilvie warned against when God's will becomes challenging. In the darkness of the fear and doubt that overwhelmed me, I questioned what God had made clear in the light.[1]

After three months, my fears and doubts appeared to be justified, for it was not going well. I had packed and unpacked my bags four different times. After one particularly rough day, I sat in the bathroom in the middle of the night with a towel pressed against my mouth. *God, you have made a mistake! Please release me from this! I don't belong here anymore. I do not love him. He does not love me. He has not forgiven me. God, how can we ever be husband and wife if I can't even bear his touch?* That night I decided that the next day I would make preparations to leave and head back to Pennsylvania, certain that God and I had made a mistake. But God had not made a mistake.

The next day, I was sitting on the living room floor struggling with a Phillips screwdriver to finish putting together a three-tiered shelf. As I worked, I felt the Holy Spirit nudge me: "Get Ogilvie's book and read again the chapter titled 'Later.'" I ignored the voice; I didn't want to hear what God had to say. I had made up my mind. I was leaving. I tightened another screw and heard, "Get the book."

This time it was compelling—so strong that I flung down the tools and cried, "Father, what do you want? What do you want from me?"

"Go and read the chapter called 'Later.' Deal with this now." I got up, went into the bedroom, picked up the book, and found the chapter. It was about the Israelites on the border of Canaan. They had arrived to the very place God had called them to, but after scouting out the land they concluded that the obstacles were too great to overcome. There were giants ahead; huge fortified cities inhabited by giant-sized men. They concluded that the risk was too great. Fear overtook them, doubt clouded their thinking, and they turned away to face the wilderness. Their fear overshadowed God's promise of future peace and pleasure. I laid the book down, and God spoke to my spirit:

You anticipated for weeks this reconciliation. You knew in your heart that I was clearly leading you here to reconcile with David. You trusted me and left your family, your home, and came to this new land of promise for your marriage. You believed that I was bringing you to a land that promises peace, love, contentment, and fulfillment with David as your husband. Then you got here and all the

*old feelings came rushing back. You look at him and recall
all the pain. You wonder how you will ever really love each
other again, how you will ever be sexually intimate again
when the very thought of it terrifies you. You wonder if you
both will ever recover from the hurt, the pain, and resent-
ment you feel. And they have become giants in your eyes,
leaving you to think that I have made a mistake or that
maybe I have not really called you to this place.*

Yet I knew deep in my heart that He had and that
He was calling me that moment to completely trust
Him and surrender to His will. In spite of all I knew,
of all I saw, and of all I felt—which was as real to me
as the giants in Canaan had been to the Israelites—
that He wanted me to press forward in total commitment and complete faithfulness to His plan, which
was reconciliation with David. Though I was caught
off-guard by the giants, God wasn't. He had called me
here even though He knew the giants existed; therefore, He must know something that I currently did
not know. He simply wanted me to surrender all to
Him—my fears, my hopes, and my dreams of what I
thought I needed to be happy—and rely only upon
Him.

But, oh, the struggle in my soul! I cannot describe the fear that gripped me; the crushing doubt.
Yet I wanted to surrender. I sank to my knees beside
the bed. I prayed and told God to break down my re-
sistance to His will and to break down the strong-

holds I had erected. Torn and suspended between my "Egyptian" past, which was empty of giants, and a future filled only with giants, I recognized what really terrified me: My only hope for happiness depended on God coming through for me. Would He? Could He? For *me*? That was the core of the issue. After all He had brought me through, after all He had delivered me from, after all the precious promises I had received from His Word, did I really think God would abandon me now? Apparently so.

I'm not any better than the Israelites, I thought as I stayed on my knees. A parting of the Red Sea, manna from heaven, water gushing from a rock wasn't enough for them to trust in the dark. They still doubted God. And they never knew! *They never knew!* They died in a wilderness, still bound in doubt and fear, never experiencing the land that flowed with milk and honey—never experiencing the reality that there are no giants that God cannot conquer or overcome! They never knew.

And for the very first time I saw it from God's perspective. I recognized it as the great tragedy it was. *And I knew that it was one I did not want to make.*

I surrendered as all these thoughts swarmed in my head. I surrendered control over my life's happiness as I prayed, *Lord, I will go forward with you; I will press on to what you have called me to do.*

My prayer took wing. It soared. I began to sense the very rightness of what I was saying in my heart. All became crystal clear—no more confusion or doubt. This is what the Father wanted, me in this place, right now, surrendering to God's plan of reconciliation. I vowed to stay and be committed and faithful regardless of the giants that had moved in with us.

This was not an easy surrender, for I made this vow in spite of wanting to run away from the hard work that was needed for healing. Though the giants were not all slain at once, that moment was a turning point. What *was* slain that day was the right to run my own life, the right to map out my own path for happiness, and the belief that God makes mistakes. God would make a way or there would be no way made at all. I pressed forward into the promised land of a restored marriage with trust and hope in a giant of a God who promised in His time to slay all the giant concerns I had about David and me, who had promised to do "exceedingly abundantly above all that we ask or think" (Eph. 3:20, NKJV).

The Milk and Honey

The next day I understood the urgency of God's command to settle it now. For that day David came to the decision that I should go back home and that he would help me move back and financially support me until I got a job. For he knew I was not happy and doubted that I could ever love him again. If I had faced him the previous day in the state I was in—firm in my decision to leave—I know that I would have turned away, packed up, and headed back east—to a wilderness of my own making.

Three years later, while in Pennsylvania for the holidays, I wrote in my journal:

> *How my life has changed! I reflected upon this as I ran the hills behind my parents' home today. Three years ago, my life was consumed with fear and sorrow. I was living with Mom and Dad, divorced, full of grief, and so lost in my life that I doubted I would ever be happy again. I recall the struggle with God's call to reconcile—to move to St. Louis and begin a new life with David. The fear and uncertainty I had as to whether we could ever love and forgive one another again hovered over me constantly like a black cloud. But today, on my run, the reality of what God has done stopped me in my tracks—for my body was racked with sobs of joy, wonder, and gratitude because God has given me back the tomorrows I had thrown away.*

In Thanksgiving 2006, we enjoyed the rare occasion of having all four of our children and our grandchildren together with us for the first time since David and I had remarried four years earlier. As we gathered around the table, I realized that right here was the "milk and honey." Right here was the fulfilled promise He had given me just before I moved to St. Louis. I had paraphrased His promise to make it personal and that is how I present it now:

Lyndell, if you walk in my ways, you shall be happy, and it shall go well with you. As David's wife, you shall be like a fruitful vine in the very heart of your home. Your children will be like olive plants all around your table and you shall see your children's children. You will reap a good marriage and a happy family if you obey me. But most of all, the peace you have longed for shall be upon you (Ps. 128:1-6, NKJV, paraphrased).

I was overwhelmed at what God had done, at His faithfulness to His word! We have a tradition of going around the table and each of us sharing what we are thankful for. When it was my turn, I shared how God had made faithful His promise. Then with tears streaming down my face, I said, "When I think of the road I could have taken four years ago, I realize that we would not be here today, all of us together as a family. My road would have created new and different roads for you. How very grateful I am today that God stooped down into my life and set me on the right road, that He gave your father back to me and has healed our marriage. Because we have put Him first, there have been numerous blessings in all our lives. *This* is what God does and will do for all of us, if we but walk in His way."

I shudder when I think how close I came to missing moments such as these and how close I came to missing the promised land of our marriage. But the greatest tragedy would have been if the fate of the Israelites and been mine and *I would never have known that there is absolutely nothing impossible with God!*

Henry Blackaby says in *Experiencing God:* "God does not ask us to dream our dreams for Him and then ask Him to join our plans. He is already at work when He comes to us. . . . When God reveals to you where He is working, that becomes His invitation to join Him."[2]

Never in my life had God revealed himself so powerfully to me as when He asked me to reconcile with David. God is passionately present in the area of reconciliation, and He longs for estranged couples to join Him. He will go to extraordinary lengths to convince you that you are on the right road. Sadly, what stops us is what stopped the Israelites in the wilderness—unbelief.

I realize that it takes two to reconcile and that there are sometimes extenuating circumstances that make reconciliation impossible. But for those who have the opportunity to reconcile, unbelief is often the tallest giant. Our vision is very small when it comes to God reconciling irreconcilable differences, and at the core of unbelief is our distrust in God's love, goodness, wisdom, and power. Can He? Will He? For *me?* Hear the Word, and let it sink deep into your soul:

- "I taught Ephraim [put your name here to make it personal] to walk, taking them by their arms; but they did not know that I healed them. I drew them with gentle cords, with bands of love, and I was to them as those who take the yoke from their neck. I stooped and fed them" (Hos. 11:3-4, NKJV).

What a beautiful image! The God of the universe loves us so much that He stoops down to feed us in the famine of our sins, and with gentle cords of love brings healing to our broken marriages. And why does He do this?

- "The LORD, the LORD God, merciful and gracious, longsuffering, and abounding in goodness and truth, keeping mercy for thousands, forgiving iniquity and transgression and sin" (Exod. 34:6-7, NKJV).

No matter the sin around us, it will never diminish God's goodness. No matter what has happened in our marriages, God is always good! Thus, we need not worry.

- "For I know the plans I have for you" (Jer. 29:11).

We can stop there, for that is all we need to know. If we believe in His goodness, then all we need to know is that He knows the plans and they will be good, and He can execute His plans because He owns all the power:

- "Indeed I have spoken it; I will also bring it to pass. I have purposed it; I will also do it" (Isa. 46:11, NKJV).

Now, in light of that:

- "You shall not dread [fill in the blank] for the LORD your God is in your midst, a great and awesome God" (Deut. 7:21, NASB).

Why? Because something of great magnitude is at stake:

- "I call heaven and earth to witness against you today, that I have set before you life and death, the blessing and the curse. So choose life in order that you may live, you and your descendants" (30:19, NASB).

Can you believe that part of the abundant life God wants to give you is tied up in a loving, genuine, and intimate relationship with your husband? Jesus implies this when the Pharisees tested Him by asking Him: "Is it lawful for a man to divorce his wife for any reason at all?" And Jesus answered, "Have you not read that He who created them from the beginning MADE THEM MALE AND FEMALE, and said, 'FOR THIS REASON A MAN SHALL LEAVE HIS FATHER AND MOTHER AND BE JOINED TO HIS WIFE, AND THE TWO SHALL BECOME ONE FLESH'?" (Matt. 19:3-5, NASB).

I read again and again those words of Jesus in the early days of our reconciliation, and one day it dawned upon me that of all the relationships God could have made in the beginning—male and mother, male and father, male and friend, male and male, male and child, male and golden retriever—God instead gave man a woman to be his wife. It was what God wanted, what He designed, what He purposed, because He knew that the joy of oneness we crave is wrapped up in each other. As I studied this passage, God spoke to my spirit, making it personal: "In the beginning, I made you, David and Lyndell. It was my design. It was my purpose; my plan. I knew that you would bring joy and fulfillment to one another. And, though, like Adam and Eve, you have made wrong and sinful choices that have prohibited that from taking place, it does not negate my original purpose and plan—for *I* made you, in the beginning, David and Lyndell, and 'what therefore God has joined together, let no man separate'" (Matt. 19:6, NASB).

This passage assured me that it was God's will for reconciliation to take place between David and me rather than continue as "separated" people. He knew that because of our stubborn willfulness, moments of great "separation" would occur—but that is never God's way nor need it be the end of the story.

I believe that God longs to show us that He is the God of the impossible when it comes to irreconcilable differences! Yet I have witnessed many who quickly and easily refuse to consider it a viable option. Besides the sin of unbelief, they simply are not willing to pay the price. What we fail to realize, however, is that reconciliation will and *should* cost us, for at the heart of God's reconciliation with us stood a cross upon which someone had to die. We cannot expect it to be any different. We cannot escape the cross that stands at the heart of reconciliation between a husband and a wife. On it, we, too, must die. Without such a sacrifice, we cannot expect to be reconciled. An "all about me" attitude will kill every effort to rebuild a marriage.

If you are willing to die to self and not leave God and His Word out of the equation, I promise you, you will see miracles occur. But more importantly, just as the cross of Christ robbed Satan of the sting of death, reconciliation robs Satan of having the last word. It restores the message that God is powerful enough to rebuild the ruin of a broken marriage. And His Word holds powerful promises to aid us when we say yes to reconciliation. We simply choose to believe or to not believe His Word. There can be no fence sitting; we cannot procrastinate when it comes to the life of our marriage.

In Ogilvie's book there was one particular story that dropped me to my knees the day I surrendered my future to God. It was about a young man whose father had retreated from the difficult challenge of making his marriage work. Rather than working through the problems, he began an affair with another woman. The son urged him to not go this route, but it was in vain. Later, the son said, "My father stood up to bat for his life. When he got one strike against him, he left the mound. With some courage, he could have hit a home run with my mom. Instead, he struck out by default . . . he procrastinated so long that he lost his nerve."[3]

Don't let your marriage die by default; don't delay because you are afraid to step out in faith and trust God's Word and thus never embrace the miracle He has in store for your marriage. If I had not settled once and for all that day that I was committed to reconciliation, then stronger, ungodly emotions would have carried me away to a tragic decision—to a place where I *knew* that one day I would discover it as a vast wilderness and would have forfeited God's greatest blessings for my life.

The now-or-never call comes to us when we must make a wholehearted commitment to stay, to reconcile, and do whatever God calls us to do. It is a call to an unshakable commitment, a steadfast faithfulness, regardless of what we feel or do not feel. When you get to this place, hear the promise He spoke to me that day by my bedside. It is also for you: "If you are willing to surrender your *self* to that level of commitment today, I will show you a level of feelings that you have never experienced before. I will show you a relationship that is alive, dynamic, full of joy and genuine love unlike you have ever known. I will bring you the peace and oneness your soul has longed for."

When Sara joined me the next day, she expressed some very legitimate fears about "forsaking all others" in order to love her husband again. I redirected her focus away from falling in love with her husband again to falling in love with Jesus again. Reconciliation must first begin with Him, the one whom we have grieved, before reconciliation can occur between others. When Jesus becomes the lover of your soul, everything else begins to correctly align itself under His Lordship. The next step is to take your fears and lay them down. Only then can you experience a new beginning.

- List your fears about reconciling—the "what if" fears you have.

- List your "what if" fears you have about God— the areas of unbelief where you feel that God could not or would not come through for you. Then write a prayer of confession about your unbelief, asking for help and forgiveness.

- Read Isa. 54. Concentrate especially on verses 11 and 12. This is what God will do for you! Write down what you think God is saying to you through His Word.

- Bundle up all your fears and concerns and give them to God. Write to Him a prayer of your commitment to reconcile with your husband and to do whatever He shows you to do.

I pray that you will yield to the Creator today who stood at the beginning of your marriage and has the love, wisdom, and power to create a golden ending. If you are willing to make such a courageous move, God will move heaven and earth to rebuild a marriage you will be so grateful to not have missed.

Lyndell would like to hear what God is doing in your life and marriage. You can reach her at LyndellHH@aol.com.

Special Prayers

Prayer for Redemption

Lord Jesus: For so long I have shut you out of my life. I have lived to please myself and others, but not you. Even though I have tried to be good and do all the right things, I have failed, for I tried to do it apart from you. I realize now that living this way is called sin, and that it has separated me from God. But I don't want to live this way any longer. I want to turn around and go in a new direction with you at the center of my life. I repent of my sins and of my selfish pursuits, and I ask for your forgiveness. I believe that you are the Christ, the Son of God, and that you died on the Cross to pay the penalty for my sin. Please come into my life and make me brand-new. Today, by the power of your grace, I will turn from following my way to following your way. Thank you, Jesus, for redeeming me from a path of futility, hopelessness, and eternal destruction. I thank you for the gifts of faith, hope, and eternal life. In your name I pray. Amen.

Signed: _____

Date: _____

Prayer for Restoration

Dear Heavenly Father: May you continue to do your healing work in my heart, mind, and soul. I invite you to reach into the deepest part of me with your truth and grace and to uncover everything that hinders my walk with you. In the Bible you are called the Wonderful and Mighty Counselor. This means that you know all about me and that you alone can heal the damage within. I can hide nothing from you. You know the shame, the painful regrets, the deceit. Help me face my pain and not run from it. Lord, I long to be made whole. Restore beauty, tranquillity, and contentedness to my soul. Restore innocence and purity to my heart and mind. Cleanse and heal me of all wasteful thoughts and memories. Bring the light of your Word into my inner being and uncover all the worldly lies I have secretly harbored. I vow to walk in obedience to all that you show me so that complete healing can take place. I vow to no longer cling to my painful and sinful past. I commit my entire life to you, to your counsel, and to your lovingkindness. In Jesus' name I pray. Amen.

Notes

Chapter 2

1. George Barna, *The Barna Update,* "Born Again Christians Just as Likely to Divorce as Are Non-Christians" (Oct. 20, 2004) <http:www.orthodoxytoday.org/articles4/BarnaDivorce.shtml>.

Chapter 3

1. Clark Pinnock, *Flame of Love: A Theology of the Holy Spirit* (Downer's Grove, Ill.: InterVarsity Press, 1966), 180.

2. Oswald Chambers, *Abandoned to God* (Grand Rapids: Discovery House Publishers, 1993), 13.

3. Oswald Chambers, *My Utmost for His Highest* (Uhrichsville, Ohio: Barbour Publishing, 1935), 153.

Chapter 4

1. Charles Spurgeon, "An Antidote to Satan's Devices," from *30 Days to Discovering Personal Victory Through Holiness* (Sisters, Oreg.: Multnomah, 2003), 174-75.

2. Gordon MacDonald, *A Resilient Life* (Nashville: Thomas Nelson, 2004), 55.

Chapter 6

1. A. W. Tozer, *Man: The Dwelling Place of God* (Camp Hill, Pa.: WingSpread Publishers, a division of Zur Ltd., 1996), 78.

2. John Wesley, *Renew My Heart* (Uhrichsville, Ohio: Barbour Publishing, 2002), 270-71.

3. C. S. Lewis, *A Year with C. S. Lewis* (San Francisco: HarperSanFrancisco, 2003), 143.

Chapter 9

1. Randy Alcorn, "Strategies to Keep from Falling," *Christianity Today, Inc.* (Aug. 3, 2006) <http://www.epm.org/articles/leadpur.htlm>.

2. *Wall Street Journal,* "Straight Talk About 'Happy Talk'" (Oct. 21, 2005).

Chapter 10

1. Peggy Vaughn, "Marriage to an Affair Partner" (Mar. 30, 2006) <http://lists101.his.com/pipermail/smartmarriages/2006-March/002981.html>.

2. Anne Kass, "Second Marriage Can Be as Difficult as the First One" (Sept. 10, 2006) <http:www.alllaw.com/articles/family/divorce/article49.asp>.

3. Daisy Goodwin, *101 Poems That Could Save Your Life* (New York: Harper Collins, 2003), 28.

4. Dr. Willard Harley, Jr., *His Needs, Her Needs: Building an Affair-Proof Marriage* (Grand Rapids: Fleming H. Revell, 1994), 16.

5. Walter Trobisch, *Living with Unfulfilled Desires* (Downer's Grove, Ill.: InterVarsity Press, 1979), 23.

Chapter 11

1. William Barclay, *The Letter to the Hebrews* (Philadelphia: Westminster Press, 1976), 154.

2. Chambers, *Abandoned to God*, 88.

3. Lysa TerKeurst, *Radically Obedient, Radically Blessed* (Eugene, Oreg.: Harvest House, 2003), 14.

Chapter 12

1. Dallas Willard, "A Divine Conspirator," *Christianity Today, Inc.* (Sept. 2006), 47.

2. Henri J. M. Nouwen, *The Wounded Healer* (Garden City, N.Y.: Doubleday and Company, Inc., 1972), 96.

3. C. S. Lewis, *Mere Christianity* (New York: Macmillan Publishing Company, Inc., 1943), 71.

4. Andrew Murray, *A Life of Obedience* (Minneapolis: Bethany House, 1982), 42.

Chapter 13

1. Lloyd John Ogilvie, *Lord of the Impossible* (Nashville: Abingdon Press, 1984), 92.

2. Henry Blackaby and Claude V. King, *Experiencing God* (Nashville: Broadman & Holman, 1994), 55.

3. Ogilvie, *Lord of the Impossible*, 92.